ISTANBUL

UĞUR AYYILDIZ
Art historian and professional guide

NET
TURİSTİK YAYINLAR
SANAYİ VE TİCARET A.Ş.

CONTENTS

Published and distributed by:

NET TURİSTİK YAYINLAR A.Ş.

Şifa Hamamı Sok. No. 18/2, 34400 Sultanahmet-İstanbul/Turchia
Tel: (90-212) 516 32 28 - 516 82 61 Fax: (90-212) 516 84 68

Mithatpaşa Cad. No. 643/B 35280 Köprü-İzmir/Turchia
Tel: (90-232) 244 86 44 - 243 57 10 Fax: (90-232) 231 84 18

Kışla Mah. 54. Sok., İlteray Apt., No. 11/A-B, 07040 Antalya/Turchia
Tel: (90-242) 248 93 67 - 243 14 97 Fax: (90-242) 248 93 68

Yeni Mahalle Saatçi Hoca Cad. Dirikoçlar Apt. No. 43 Nevşehir/Turchia
Tel: (90-384) 213 30 89 - 213 46 20 Fax: (90-384) 213 40 36

Photographs: **Tahsin Aydoğmuş, Güngör Özsoy, Haluk Özözlü, Erdal Yazıcı**

Layout: **Kemal Özdemir**

Typesetting: **AS & 64 Ltd. Şti.**

Printed in Turkey by: **Keskin Color Ltd. Şti. Matbaası**

ISBN 975-479-154-6

Copyright © 1995 NET TURİSTİK YAYINLARI A.Ş.

2001

WELCOME TO ISTANBUL

Istanbul, once a city that aroused the curiosities of travellers as the centre of the world, is a metropolis where Eastern and Western civilizations meet. In the city, the contemporary western way of life exists together with the traditional. Modern buildings and art forms appear side by side with classical Turkish, Byzantine and Roman masterpieces. Istanbul is the largest city in Turkey, owing largely to its status as the most active trade, import and export, industrial, entertainment and educational centre of the country. The climate in Istanbul is mild and the landscape, with sea and land intermingling in delicate harmony, is beautiful.

The Bosphorus is beautiful year round, even in the rainy - and occasionally snowy - days of the winter. Spring, with its different shades of green and blossoming trees is rather short and the month of May marks the beginning of summer in Istanbul. Also in May thousands of travellers from all

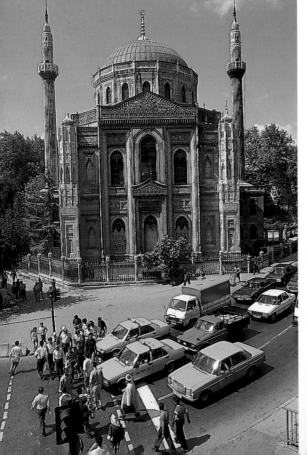

parts of the world begin pouring in to enjoy the beauty and the historical riches of the city.

Summer in Istanbul means rushing to the beaches. There are not many cities in the world that offer as great a choice as does Istanbul in variety of places for swimming. Both the cool waters of the Black Sea and the splendid warm beaches of the Princes'Islands are easily reached from the city centre by short cruises. On the shores of the Bosphorus as well as the Sea of Marmara are numerous public beaches with facilities. The long autumn, when the skies are clear and the temperatures are moderate, is especially suitable for tourism.

Turkish cuisine is also an experience not to be missed. (The Turkish kitchen is one of the three major culinary schools of the world.) Fresh fruits and vegetables of unbelievable variety appear on the menus especially in spring, summer and autumn, and fresh fish from the Black Sea, the Bosphorus and the Sea of Marmara is a treat to palates mistreated elsewhere.

TOURS OF THE CITY

Historic Istanbul cannot be separated from the Bosphorus and the Golden Horn, by the shores of which it was first founded. There are not many places in the world where wonders of nature and masterpieces of man mix so gracefully, and where the testimony of the past is seen as vividly, as in Istanbul. The visitor who tours this magnificent city carries home unforgettable memories. The daily tours offered by local travel agencies usually enable the visitor staying for a short time to see the principal spots of interest in the city such as the Hagia Sophia Museum, the Süleymaniye Mosque, the Blue Mosque, the Hippodrome, the Topkapı Palace and the Covered Bazaar and its surroundings. In addition to these classical tours, there are many other tours of prominent Roman, Byzantine and Turkish sites in the city, as well as along the Asian and European shores of the Bosphorus. These daily tours depart from hotels or

the port and last for half a day or a full day giving the visitor a general overview of Istanbul. However, if the visitor wishes to see all there is to be seen in Istanbul, more time is necessary. Then the visitor can explore the Roman city walls, the renowned Kariye Museum, with its late Byzantine frescoes and mosaics, the Dolmabahçe Palace on the Bosphorus which is regarded as the richest palace in the world, the Spice Market, the Galata Tower, the Archaeological Museum and the Turkish and Islamic Arts Museum.

An Istanbul evening tour with belly-dancing and folk shows is a night straight from the Thousand and One Nights.

A visit to Istanbul may provide some travellers with the oportunity of setting foot in Asia for the first time, since there are daily tours either by boat or across the Bosphorus Bridge that joins the two continents. It is in course of these tours, especially while crossing the bridge or during a repose at Çamlıca Hill that one gets to see the city in its total magnificence.

ORIENTATION

The historic city of Istanbul was originally founded on the seven hills of a peninsula surrounded on its three sides by the Sea of Marmara, the Bosphorus and its arm called the Golden Horn. The location was ideal for many reasons. It was centrally located on East-West trade routes, easily defendable with only one landward side, it dominated the well-protected 8 km. long natural harbour of the Golden Horn, which was surrounded by fertile and abounding in game, and the climate was mild year round. Hence, the city kept growing gradually and from the 4th century A.D. on, was regarded as the centre of the old world since it was the capital of one empire after another (namely the Roman, Byzantine and Ottoman empires in succession) for about 1.600 years, a capital where over 120 emperors and sultans reigned.

Throughout its history, the old city kept growing westwards on the peninsula, and accordingly that segment of the city walls was rebuilt four times. The last line, which can still be seen today, was built in the 5th century A.D. and had stood against the assaults of many conquerors before giving in to the Ottoman Army of Sultan Mehmed II in 1453.

Under Ottoman rule, the city began to change. Since there was no longer the threat of any enemy reaching the capital of the powerful empire, new settlements on the Asian as well as the European coasts of the Bosphorus developed and also on the hills across the Golden Horn a Genoese colony emerged at a spot called Galata. The skyline of the city changed significantly. The fine minarets of imperial mosques that are regarded as the crown of Istanbul began rising immediately after the conquest of the city.

Left: Kabataş Pier.
Kartal Coast, Looking at Bosphorus from Dolmabahçe.

Right: Merit Antique Hotel, Laleli.
Kumkapı: One of the locations famous for its lively night life.

Bird's-eye view of the historical peninsula.

Today, Istanbul is the largest city of modern Turkey, and with its 7 million inhabitants, one of the most crowded European cities. In the old city that has expanded beyond the city walls since the end of the 19th century, most of the main road and squares are still the same as they had been in the 5th and 6th centuries. Most of the important buildings - palaces, places of worship, etc. - of the Byzantine and Ottoman periods and even some of those of the Roman period still stand intact. Most of the narrow streets and peculiar apartment houses of Galata and Beyoğlu, where the Christian population of the city used to dwell, still look the same as they did at the turn of the century. The European architectural style of some 80-90 years ago may be observed in the upper part of the hill where the embassies of European countries had been.

Nowadays, this area is surrounded by modern hotels, trade centres and residential quarters.

The hills on the two sides of the Bosphorus are covered with woods. The shores are adorned with magnificient palaces, mosques, summer residences of certain embassies to the Ottoman Empire and the two fortresses. Also, contemporary buildings blend into the predominately historic view of the Bosphorus. Because people tend to prefer eating and drinking amidst beautiful scenery, restaurants and taverns serving fresh seafood and other "mezes" (Turkish, Hors d'oeuvres) line both shores.

The Bosphorus currents which posed a great challenge to the sailboats and rowboats in the old times, today, carry the dense traffic between Black Sea ports and the rest of the world. On a tour of the Bos-

12

phorus, the most dominant sight is of course the Bosphorus Bridge. Built in 1973, the bridge has reduced to minutes the time needed for motor vehicles to cross the strait. Today, about one third of the population of Istanbul resides in the Asian part of the city. Here, the major points of attraction are several beautiful mosques in Üsküdar; the Barracks of Selimiye, which while serving as a military hospital during the Crimean War, witnessed the heroic work of Florence Nightingale, founder of modern nursing; and the twin hills of Çamlıca offering the eye the best panoramic view of Istanbul. Also in the vicinity is the Karacaahmet Cemetery.

Another important part of Istanbul is the Princes'Islands, an archipelago of nine islands and islets in the Sea of Marmara. There are many summer houses and seaside mansions on the four larger Islands where no motor vehicles are allowed. The only means of transportation is the horsedrawn phaetons.

The Sea of Marmara, known as the "smallest sea in the world" is connected to the Black Sea through the Strait of Bosphorus and to the Aegean through the Strait of Dardanelles. It is exceptionally rich in fish and sea flora.

HISTORY

Turkey is a land of historic treasures. No other land in the world has as bountiful historic treasures as Turkey, a land also of many unique wonders of nature. Situated as a bridge between two continents, the subcontinent called Anatolia or Asia Minor which constitutes the larger part of the country, has been regularly inhabited by man since the prehistoric ages and has witnessed the flourishing of many of the ancient civilizations known today. Thousands of archaeological sites have been discovered in Turkey and, some of them date back to the 9th millenium B.C..

Of the two ancient settlements near the twin straits that mark the western frontiers of Anatolia, namely the ancient city of Troy near the Strait of Dardanelles (Hellespont) and the city of Istanbul on both sides of the Strait of Bosphorus, the former is just a famous ruin nowadays, whereas the latter is still living, more lively than ever.

The highlight of the history of the smaller

European part of Turkey is the history of Istanbul. There are many legends about the foundation of the city. The most famous of these goes as follows: At about 650 B.C. a tribe of seafarers decided to leave their home - a city called Megara - under the guidance of their leader Byzas, to search for a new homeland. It was customary then to consult soothsayers before doing anything. The soothsaying priests told him that they should settle at a place "facing the land of the blind". Byzas and his people set sail and after a long and exhausting search in many seas, came to the peninsula of Istanbul. They immediately admired the beauty and bounty lying before them and noticed the possibilites offered by the gulf now called the Golden Horn.

They also spotted a colony of people living across the strait and Byzas ruled "if people who have come this close to a piece of land so suitable for settlement fail to see its virtues, they must be blind" and hence they build on the peninsula the foundations of the city we now call Istanbul.

On the other hand, traces of settlement which date back to about 3rd millenium B.C. have been uncovered in excavations near the apex of the Golden Horn and in the Asiatic part of the city.

ROMAN PERIOD

For a few centuries following its establishment, Istanbul existed as a sea port and centre for trade, sovereign for certain periods and under the control of superior powers dominating the region the rest of the time. In this period, the city had its acropolis at the site where the Topkapı Palace stands today, and a busy port was situated at the well-sheltered entrance of the Golden Horn.

The strong city walls started at the port and, running along the outskirts of the settlement, reached the Sea of Marmara. Istanbul remained so during the rule of the Roman Empire until the year 191 A.D. when the city took sides with what apparently was

Above: Jesus Christ (Hagia Sophia Museum). Aqueduct of Valens in Saraçhane. The city walls of Istanbul (below).

14

the wrong party in a dispute over the throne of the empire. After a siege that lasted for more than two years, it was conquered and razed to the ground by the Roman Emperor Septimius Severus.

The city was later rebuilt and expanded by the same emperor with new city walls and many new buildings. In the 4th century, the Pax Romana had expanded over such a wide area that the city of Rome, its capital, was no longer centrally located.

Emperor Constantine the Great who realized the difficulty in ruling such a vast land from Rome recognized the advantages offered by Istanbul's location at the crossroads of the major land and sea routes of the time and its mild climate, and named the city his new capital.

This triggered rapid development in the city. A new line of city walls were built in about six years so that the city could expand easily, and a number of temples, palaces, official buildings, baths and a hippodrome were constructed. In 330 A.D. with great fanfare, the city was officially proclaimed the capital of the Roman Empire.

During the golden age that, the city was first called Deutera Roma (the Second Rome) or Nea Roma (the New Rome), but these two names were soon given up and replaced by Byzantium which was used for many centuries until "Constantinopolis" (or "Polis" for short among the common folk) became popular.

The emperors succeeding Constantine carried on with the effort to beautify and improve the city and built new buildings, avenues, aqueducts and monuments. The first churches in the city were also constructed during this period.

BYZANTINE PERIOD

In the year 395, the great Roman Empire was divided into two parts. The Western Empire collapsed soon afterwards - in the 5th century - whereas the Eastern Empire, called the Byzantine Empire by contemporary historians, continued to exist for more than a thousand years. The Byzantine Empire grew under the influence of earlier Anatolian civilizations with structures and codes adopted from the East. It had its roots in the Roman Empire and most important of all, it was under the influence of Christianity. In the first half of the 5th century, during the reign of Emperor Theodosius II, the boundaries of the city were enlarged again, and the 6492 metre-long city walls that still stand today in all their magnificence were built. These walls that were constructed as two parallel lines of fortifications with a deep moat on the outside are known to have stopped numerous attacks.

In the 6th century, the city and its population of more than half a million enjoyed another golden age of prosperity and progress under Emperor Justinian. The Church of Hagia Sophia, Byzantine most imposing place of worship that still stands today, was built during his reign. The city was restructured with all the major avenues starting at the church and running towards the city

Above: Empress Zoe (Hagia Sophia Museum). Page 16: Teodosius I. his family and the administrators (A detail from the relief of the Teodosius I. obelisk) (above) The Tekfur Palace (below).

walls, branching into two at some of the important squares.

The history of the Byzantine Empire and that of the city of Istanbul after Justinian is filled with palace and church intrigue, Persian and Arab attacks and bloody power struggles that often resulted in the replacement of dynasties. During the Iconoclastic movement between the years 726 and 842, the use of icons was denounced.

The Latin invasion of the city that began in 1204 in the course of the Fourth Crusade is a dismal chapter in the history of Istanbul. The strong and battle-ready crusader army had little problem in conquering the city and immediately began robbing it of its treasures. The looting went on for many years and included even such holy places as churches and monasteries. When the invasion ended in 1261, the city was stripped of everything valuable and could never become the prosperous city it once was, up until its siege and eventual conquest by the Ottomans in 1453.

OTTOMAN PERIOD

Superior guns of large caliber were used for the first time in history by Sultan Mehmed II (later to be called Sultan Mehmed, the Conqueror) during the siege that lasted for 53 days. The twenty-one year old conqueror immediately moved the capital of the Ottoman Empire to Istanbul, and after increasing the population by moving in immigrants from the other parts of the empire, launched a campaign to repair and restore the city. In the meantime, he granted freedom of religion and other rights to the non-Moslems of the city. Some of the desolate churches including the Hagia Sophia were repaired and converted to mosques.

Due to the rights granted to non-Moslems by Mehmed the Conqueror that the Patriarchate of the Christian Orthodox Church is still in Istanbul and that a large non-Moslem population still lives in the city and elsewhere in the country.

After the Turkish takeover of Istanbul, the city once again became a major city in the East, and hundred years after the conquest, the unmistakable lines of Turkish art had become prevalent in the city, and the elegant silhouettes of minarets and domes dominated the skyline.

The Ottoman Empire that developed from a small Turkish tribe into a powerful international hegemony controlling parts of Europe, Asia and Africa had Istanbul as its capital through the remainder of its existence. Furthermore, after the Ottoman Sultans assumed the title and powers of the Caliph (Successor to the Prophet Mohammed) the city of Istanbul was regarded the capital of the Islamic World, too.

Throughout the reigns of various Sultans succeeding Mehmed the Conqueror, the efforts to improve Istanbul continued. In the colourful pages of the history of Istanbul covering that period there is no record of any wars in or near the city. However, there are records of frequent great fires that destroyed large sections of the city.

The imperial palace was located at the site of the ancient acropolis which offered

Above: Sultan Mehmed, the Conqueror.   *Page 19: The reception of Barbaros Hayreddin by - Süleyman the Magnificent.*

an incredibly beautiful view of the Sea of Marmara and the Bosphorus. The palace, known by the name Topkapı, served for about four hundred years as the residence of Sultans as well as the administrative headquarters of the empire. Later on, in the 19th century, palaces and mansions began to be built, in the European architectural style on the coast of the Bosphorus. These palaces, built within a short time, are regarded by many as symbols of the decline of the Ottoman Empire.

TURKISH REPUBLIC

The decline of the Empire proved irreversible, and in the years following the end of World War I, the historic city that once was Byzantium witnessed the end of another great empire. However, the end of the Ottoman Empire did not mean the end of the determination of the Turkish people to live as an independent nation on the land which they made their home for more than nine centuries. While the victors of the World War were engaged in a heated debate among themselves over the way Turkish land would be split, a noble commander of the Ottoman Army, Mustafa Kemal, left Istanbul for Anatolia (partly occupied already) with the purpose of kindling the fire of independence. The fire he started spread rapidly to cover the whole country, and after a four-year struggle supported by almost no resources except willpower and determination, cannons in Istanbul and all around the country were fired on October 29, 1923 to celebrate the foundation of the Republic of Turkey.

From then on, the first president of the very first republic in Asia, now given the surname Atatürk ("Father of the Turks"), led the country on the path towards western civilization. This new phase in the history of Turkey included among other things, the expatriation of the last Sultan and the imperial family, the adoption of the Latin alphabet, the abolishment of the Caliphate and the prohibiton of such garments of eastern origin as the fez and veiled dress. By the time Atatürk died in 1938, Turkey was recognized as a member of the western world. Although the capital of the new republic was Ankara, Istanbul still remained the most important and the largest city of modern Turkey and maintained its enchanting look and its vivacious way of life.

Turkey is a Nato member and is ruled by a parliamentary democracy. Anatolia, the Bosphorus and the Dardanelles, because of their unusually strategic locations, are the most important points of defence of the Western world.

In modern Turkey where giant dams generate electricity, and large irrigation systems water the fertile plains, many varieties of grain, fruit and vegetables are grown. The most developed industry in the country is the textile industry (cotton, silk and vool). Every kind of cereal and industrial product is exported to many contries from the modern ports in the country.

Above: Mustafa Kemal Atatürk (1881-1938), the founder of Turkish Republic. Right: A view from national holiday celebrations. The Bosphorus Bridge , inaugurated in the 50th year of the republic.

THE CITY HIPPODROME

The "Hippodrome" (horse race-track) was built in the 2nd century during the reign of the Roman emperor Septimius Severus, and was expanded to colossal dimensions under Constantine the Great. Some historians record the seating capacity of this huge arena as 30,000 and some even go as high as 60,000.

The Hippodrome, during the Roman and Byzantine empires was the centre for entertainment, amusement and sports in the city. Two or 4-horse chariot races highlighted each day's programme which also featured performances by groups of musicians, dancers, acrobats and animal trainers. Especially, during the Roman empire, when holidays were numerous, people had ample leisure time and spent most of it at the Hippodrome.

The Hippodrome was U-shaped and the Emperor's box, with four bronze statues of horses on its roof, was located by the eastern stretch of the track. A low wall separated the two stretches and also served as a podium for mementoes brought from all around the empire, and for the statues of famous chariot drivers and horses. In those days, a chariot race winner was regarded as a public hero and came to possess all the riches conceivable. Therefore, the chariot drivers competed with all their might, sometimes employing the most ruthless tactics to win. They were divided into teams of "Blues", "Greens", "Reds", etc. and their fans even had political power. This inter-mixture of sport and politics sometimes led to curious events such as street fights and even massacres triggered just by the humiliation of one of the teams (or, more appropriately, political parties) in a chariot race.

For centuries, the Hippodrome stood intact and remained as most important landmarks in the Byzantine city. But, after the invasion of the Crusaders in 1204, it was stripped of almost all the monuments that

Sultanahmet Square (Hippodrome).

once adorned it and eventually destroyed.

Later, during the Ottoman rule of the city, the Hippodrome grounds were used occasionally for festivities and ceremonies that were reminiscent of its early times.

What is left of this once magnificient arena is the racing track - or rather the outline of it - with the surface filled to a level 4 - 5 metres above the original, and only three monuments: Two obelisks and the Serpentine Column.

The Egyptian Obelisk:

This obelisk made of exceptionally high quality pink granite was originally erected around 1490 B.C. by the Pharaoh Tuthmosis III at a spot in front of the Temple of Karnak at Luxor to commemorate the victories of his armies in Mesopotamia. It was brought to Istanbul during the fourth century upon orders of a Roman emperor not yet identified clearly, who wished to stage an event that would demonstrate his power and hence excite and impress his people.

The obelisk was left lying at one corner of the Hippodrome for a long time until the year 390 during the reign of Theodosius I when it was erected with great difficulty by Proclus, one of the administrators of the city. This obelisk, the most ancient monument of Istanbul, was always considered, magical.

The obelisk stands on four bronze cubes placed on a Roman base adorned with reliefs depicting the Emperor, his family and other important people watching the races from the imperial box as well as the people, musicians, dancers and chariot races. The height of the obelisk, with its base, is 25.60 metres from ground level.

The Walled Obelisk:

At the southern end of the Hippodrome stands the imitation obelisk built out of roughly shaped pieces of Stone. The exact

Egyptian Obelisk and Serpentine Column.

24

date it was built is not known. The monument is named after Emperor Constantine Porphyrogenetus who had it repaired in the 10th century. The bronze plates that used to cover its surfaces were stripped during the Fourth Crusade.

The Serpentine Column:

The Serpentine Column is one of the most ancient monuments in Istanbul. It was originally the base of a golden cauldron. The heads of three serpents whose bodies are twined in a column provided the three points on which the cauldron rested. The 8-metre column and the cauldron were made of bronze. The bronze items captured by 31 Greek cities when they defeated the Persians in the 5th century B.C. were melted and used to make the column and the cauldron which was erected at the Temple of Apollo in Delphi.

In 324 A.D., Emperor Constantine the Great had it carried to Istanbul and erected at the Hippodrome. According to many sources, the heads of the serpents were still intact by the early 1700's, but were broken afterwards. Later, one of the heads was found and placed in the Istanbul Archaeological Museum.

The German Fountain:

The octagonal, domed fountain at the entrance of the Hippodrome was a gift from the German Emperor Wilhelm II to Sultan Abdülhamid II and the City of Istanbul. It was made in Germany and installed at its present site in Istanbul in 1898. The dome of the fountain, designed in the neo-Byzantine style, is decorated with golden mosaics.

Although a beautiful piece of art, the German Fountain poses a contrast to the ancient monuments that surround it.

The Walled Obelisk and The German Fountain.

25

The Museum of Turkish and Islamic Arts.

THE MUSEUM OF TURKISH AND ISLAMIC ARTS

Since 1983, the museum has occupied the 16th century building situated along the western side of Sultanahmet Square (the Hippodrome). The building used to be the palace of İbrahim Paşa. Apart from the imperial palaces, it is the only extant private palace. The edifice surrounds the three sides of a terrace, forming a courtyard in the middle.

Following the entrance, the first section of the museum is reached by a staircase from the courtyard. Rare ancient works of art created in various Islamic lands are on

A tile wall panel depicting the Kaaba.

Sewing box.

display in the hallways and in the rooms. Stone and baked clay objets, ceramic and glassware, and handwritten books are some of the most valuable examples of their period. The carpets exhibited in the large halls occupying the section of the building with wide windows in the facade, are magnificent examples of the famous 13th-20th century hand-knotted Turkish carpets. This matchless collection is the richest of its kind in the world. The 13th century Seljouk carpets and rare examples from the following centuries are restored and exhibited with much care.

A safe for the Koran.

THE SULTAN AHMED MOSQUE (THE BLUE MOSQUE)

The Sultan Ahmed Mosque, one of the most revered masterpieces not only of Turkey but of the Islamic World as well, inspires deep admiration in all those who visit it. It is a striking example of classical mosques built with six minarets. The mosque is surrounded by many monuments dating back to the earlier phases of the history of Istanbul, and its fine silhouette is a prominent part of the beautiful skyline of Istanbul as seen from the sea.

Although built between 1609 and 1616 by Sultan Ahmed I (and named after him), the mosque is known throughout the world as "the Blue Mosque" owing to the dominant colour of the paint and the ceramic tiles used generously to decorate its interior. The architect designed and built the mosque as the core of a complex consisting of such functional buildings as a covered bazaar, a Turkish bath, a public kitchen for the poor, a hospital, schools, a caravansarai, and later the tomb of Sultan Ahmed I. Unfortunately, some of these structures have not survived to this day.

The main entrance to the mosque is on the side facing to the ancient Roman hippodrome and opens onto the outer court that surrounds a podium upon which the main structure and the inner court are situated. Through the door that opens to the inner court, above the diminutive ablution fountain and the colonnade that surrounds the main building, one can see the series of cupolas that rise in beautiful harmony. Upon entrance through one of the three entrances to the main building, one is impressed immediately by the colourful decor of hand-painted ceramic tiles and stained-glass windows. The interior space of the mosque exhibits perfect harmony. The central cupola and the four spherical semidomes are supported by broken arches and four thick,

The Sultan Ahmed Mosque.

Interior views of the Sultan Ahmed Mosque.

The Sultan Ahmed Mosque.

grooved pillars. The central cupola of the mosque is 23.50 m. in diameter and its height at the keystone is 43 m. The walls of the galleries on three sides of the nave are covered by more than 20,000 magnificient handmade tiles from İznik. The higher parts of the walls and the inner surfaces of the cupolas are decorated with paint. The colour of the original paint used was not blue. It was only in one of the later repairs that the colour that earned the mosque its name was applied to the walls and work is being carried on since the late 1970's to remove the dominant blue paint that was not there originally and restore the mosque's interior to its original appearance. The floor of the mosque is covered, in conformity with tradition, by carpets donated. In the wall facing the entrance are the mihrab (the prayer niche in the wall facing the Kaaba in Mecca) and the minber (pulpit) which is carved beatifully out of white marble. To the left of

the mihrab is the Sultan's box which looks like a balcony. The interior of the mosque is illuminated by natural light through 260 windows.

The cupolas, semi-domes and arches that reflect the exterior form of the mosque to the interior are decorated with paint. The mural inscriptions, every line in itself a product of great artistic effort, are verses from the Koran. Sun rays stealing in through the windows at different angles at different times of the day add colour to this beautiful monuments. As seen from the land side, the Sultan Ahmed Mosque with its system of cupolas and semidomes has the apperance of a pyramid rising over a base of horse chestnut and plane trees. The fact that the number of its minarets was equal to that of the mosque at the Holy Kaaba, at the time, caused some criticism from Moslem clergy, and Sultan Ahmed solved the problem by helping raise a seventh minaret for

The Sultan Ahmed Mosque.

the mosque in Mecca. The balconies on the minarets are reached by a spiral staircase. In older days, "müezzins" used to climb these balconies five times a day to call the believers to the mosque for prayers at the proper times. Nowadays, public-address systems are used for this purpose.

From the Asian coast at the entrance of the Bosphorus, the skyline of Istanbul at summer sunset has a fairy tale quality, offering the viewer a unique and memorable experience. Winter brings Istanbul occasional snowfall. The view of numerous cupolas under snow gives the city's monuments an entirely different look.

The rules of Islam dictate that every good Moslem practice namaz (Moslem prayer) five times a day. When they hear the call to prayer, chanted at minarets by the müezzins, believers perform ablution and rush to the mosques. The noon prayer on Fridays, morning prayers twice a year on

religious holidays, the last prayer of the month of Ramadan as well as funeral prayers must be practiced in the mosques with the congregation, whereas all other prayers may be practiced at the designated times at any suitable place. The mass prayers in the mosques are led by imams who recite verses from the Koran.

During prayers in the mosques, women and men occupy separate quarters; while men pray at the front and centre, women sit at the back and the sides. The classical Turkish mosques are structured to permit most believers in the congregation to see the mihrab even on the most crowded days. While the higher parts of the walls of the Sultan Ahmed Mosque are decorated with paint, the walls of those galleries reserved for women are covered by beautiful ceramic tiles, made specially for the mosque upon orders of the Sultan.

THE MUSEUM OF CARPETS AND KILIMS

The Administration of Pious Foundations of the Turkish Republic owns an extensive collection of old carpets and kilims, but only a part of this collection is displayed.

The carpets are exhibited in the Sultan's Pavilion in the Sultan Ahmed Mosque, and the kilims in the vaulted lower galleries entered through the rear gardens of the mosque. The best examples of 13th-20th century Turkish carpets are exhibited along the ramp which is the entrance to the pavilion, and in the rooms where the Sultan used to rest. The carpets and kilims on display have been restored and are displayed in a contemporary fashion.

The Carpets and Kilims Museum and old carpet exhibited in the Museum.

THE MOSAIC MUSEUM

The marketplace behind the Sultan Ahmed Mosque is situated on the remains of an old palace dated between the 4th and 6th centuries.

The mosaics of the palace were discovered at the lower edge of the market, in their original places. It is known that these mosaics, unearthed in the 1930's, used to decorate the floor of a large hall in the palace.

Various hunting scenes, scenes from everyday life and impressive decorative designs exhibit high quality workmanship. Buds encircled by bent acanthus leaves, a Medusa head and scenes from a lion hunt are some of the most attractive examples. Scenes depicted by these mosaic panels, created in the style of Antakya Mosaic School (Roman Age), are extremely realistic.

Following the discovery of these mosaics, other mosaics unearthed in other sections of the city were framed by concrete panels and brought here to be displayed. Restoration of the market place has been completed and the Mosaic Museum has been reopened to the public.

Three mosaic panels exhibited in the Mosaic Museum.

Aerial view of the Hagia Sophia Museum.

The Mosaic panel Christ (detail).

THE HAGIA SOPHIA MUSEUM

The Hagia Sophia, nominated by many authors and historians as one of the eighth wonders of the world, is certainly a masterpiece of architecture since it is one of the few structures of such huge dimensions to have stood erect for so long. Its architectural mastery was far ahead of its time and unmatched for 1000 years.

Originally, the name Hagia Sophia (Ayasofya in Turkish) was mistranslated as Saint Sophia. The basilica was not dedicated to a saint named Sophia, but rather to Holy Wisdom, and the two smaller basilicas built earlier at the same site where once stood a pagan temple, had borne the same name. The first Hagia Sophia, a small structure with a wooden roof, was constructed during the second half of the 4th century upon the orders of Constantius, son of Con-

stantine the Great. Although some sources attribute the honour to the father, it is not possible to take this claim seriously, for there is clear evidence that no house of worship was built during his reign. The first Basilica of Hagia Sophia burned down completely in a fire in the year 404, and the second basilica, which was of somewhat larger dimensions, was built in 415. It served Christians for more than a century until 532 when, in the course of an uprising against the government of Emperor Justinian (Nika Revolt) that ended in the death of ten thousand and the destruction of many buildings, it, too, was burned down.

Justinian, who was able to suppress the uprising with great difficulty, ordered that a temple "like nothing seen before since the day of Adam or can be seen in the future" be built immediately on the remains of the second Hagia Sophia. He made all the necessary means available to the architect An-

themius of Tralles and the mathematician Isidorus of Miletos who were to prepare the plans and supervise the construction, and placed all the riches of the state treasury at the disposal. Finally in 537, the largest church of the Christian world was dedicated among great festivities.

The general plan of Hagia Sophia was actually same as that which had been used before in many basilicas. However, this did not make things any easier in designing the dome. By the 6th century, a system devised earlier by Roman architects for covering large cylindrical structures with a single dome was available to the architects, but a huge, centrally located circular cupola on top of a rectangular structure was to be tried for the first time. Work progressed while monks kept chanting prayers seeking Holy protection. Numerous marble pieces and columns of different shapes and sizes dating back to more ancient times were brought in from ruins all around the empire and used in the building. There are many stories about the origin of these materials, especially the columns, but none of these can be taken seriously.

As said before, the Hagia Sophia was conceived and built by Justinian merely as a prestige building. Nevertheless for centuries, it was regarded with awe as a holy symbol, for it was not plausible for the people in those days that such a building of a size unsurpassable for about a thousand years and one that would require enormous resources and a technology much more advanced than what they were accustomed to could be built without the assistance of supernatural powers.

Although it was created during the 6th century as a Byzantine tectonic work, Hagia Sophia is actually an experiment in the Roman tradition of architecture which had no archetype and which could not be imitated afterwards. The contrast between the exterior and interior of the building as well as the colossal dome are legacies of the Roman era. The exterior is not finelined, and the constituent elements are not well proportioned. In other words, the exterior was treated simply as a crust or shell, and does not fit properly with the interior that has the magnificience of a palace, a grandeur becoming an imperial building. This bit of criticism on outlook not withstanding, the Hagia Sophia was a great achievement especially at the time it was built, and it must have been the magnitude of his achievement that excited Emperor Justinian during the basilica's dedication to the point of driving his chariot into the building and after praising the Lord for judging him worthy of such an achievement, shouting that he had surpassed King Solomon. The basilica soon developed into a religious centre with the monasteries that surrounded it within a few years, and was ready to be the scene of the perpetual struggle between the Byzantine Emperors and the Eastern Church.

Despite its uniqueness and magnificence, the building had many structural problems. The most important of these was that of statics. At the time the Hagia Sophia was built, the architectural means of transferring the weight of the cupola to the foundation were not yet fully developed. Consequently, the walls that kept slanting outwards, finally witnessed the collapse of the cupola in the year 558. While rebuilding, the cupola was raised further and the diameter reduced in order to decrease the outward thrust and stress. However this cupola, too, did not prove perfect and sections of it collapsed in the 10th and 14th centuries.

Throughout its lifetime, the maintenance of the Hagia Sophia always cost the rulers of the city vast sums and the poverty that prevailed towards the end of the Byzantine Empire left the church virtually a ruin. It was the conquest of Istanbul by Turks under Sultan Mehmed the Conqueror and the eventual conversion of the Hagia Sophia into a mosque that saved this beautiful monument. The most vital repairs were done in the 16th century by Turkish architect Sinan the Great, who, among other things, added buttresses that have supported the whole structure to this day. Also, a major restora-

An interior view of the Hagia Sophia Museum.

Virgin Mary and the Christ - Child, Emperor Comnenus II and Empress Irene.

tion was carried on in the 19th century by the Fosatti brothers. After 1926, it was repaired many times by different Turkish architects, who have also added an iron frame to the dome.

After serving for 916 years as a basilica and 477 years as a place of worship to two religions believing in the same God, the Hagia Sophia was converted into a museum upon Atatürk's orders.

The entrance of the museum is the original portal that began to be used after many centuries. Before entering, one can see the remnants of the second Hagia Sophia. Then comes the outer narthex which used to be the only part of the church where the unbaptized were admitted. This narthex is connected by five doors to the interior narthex which in turn opens by nine doors to the nave. The higher door in the middle was reserved for the entrance of the Emperor. The 9th century, mosaic panel above the

middle door, that depicts a kneeling emperor interceding for mercy before Jesus Christ sitting on a throne. On the medallions on each side are portraits of Virgin Mary and the Archangel Gabriel. The other non-figurative mosaics on the ceiling of the interior nathex are originals from the era of Justinian. Upon entering the nave, the visitors are impressed by its vastness and magnificence. Especially the dome which appears to hang unsupported from the sky, has the most striking effect. The walls are highly colourful with the beautiful marble plates used to decorate them. The three different colour tones of the mosaics on the dome indicate the three major repairs it has gone through in the past. The dome of the Hagia Sophia, with is diameter and height, is among the largest in the world. (As a result of numerous repairs, the central cupola no longer has the shape of a perfect circle - Its diameter is 31.87 m./104.5 ft. in the North - South and

Emperor Constantin Monumachus IV., Christ and Empress Zoe.

30.87 m./101.5 ft. in the East-West elevations. The height of its apex is 55.60 m./182.5 ft. from the floor.) On the two sides of the large (74.67 x 69.80 m./245 x 229 ft.) nave are two aisles that are normally dark. The interior of the Hagia Sophia is illuminated naturally through windows high on the walls. The building has 107 columns at the ground level and in the galleries. The antique porphyry columns at the corners, the central columns made of green broccia of Salonika and their white marble capitals rich in carved designs take the visitor back to ancient times. To enjoy a visit to the Hagia Sophia fully, one should try to imagine the place as the church or mosque it used to be and feel the magnificently mystical air that inspired feelings of awe in believers. During the period when the Hagia Sophia was the cathedral of a great and prosperous empire, the chancel, the ivory altar and the ambones were veneered by gold and silver

plates and ornamented with jewels. The sacred articles used during the rites were also made of precious metals and stones, and even some of the doors were decorated with the same. All these items were looted and carried to Europe during the invasion of the city in the curse of the Fourth Crusade.

The large circular leather pendants 7.5 m. in diameter, suspended from the walls at the gallery level, and the inscription inside the central cupola are reminders of the fact that the building was also used as a mosque. The Arabic inscriptions on the pendants as well as in the cupola, are the creations of the most famous artisans of the 19th century and are among the best examples of this branch of art. The mihrab (prayer niche) and the minber (pulpit) in the apse of the church as well as the chanters' balcony are later additions. On the other hand, the square shaped area paved with pieces of coloured marble just in front of the chant-

Virgin Mary, Christ and St. John the Baptist.

ers' balcony is probably from the 12th century, and marks the place where the emperors were to stand while being crowned. The Perspiring Column stands in the northern corner of the nave and a bronze belt surrounds its lower section. The column has a finger-hole in its body and there are many stories about it. Of the buttresses that support the structure, the one at the north has a ramp inside which provides easy ascent to the upper galleries. The magnificent view of the nave is especially impressive from these galleries that surround the nave at three sides. During the days of the Byzantine Empire, parts of these galleries were reserved for the ladies of the court and the rest was used by the congregation. On the wall of the northern gallery, there is a single mosaic mural while the wall of the southern gallery is adorned with other murals, each depicting three holy personalities. The large mosaic panel seen while leaving the museum through the interior narthex is a work of art from the 10th century. The central figure in this panel with a distorted perspective is the Virgin Mary with the infant Jesus on her knees. To her sides are Emperor Justinian presenting them with the model of Hagia Sophia. The colossal doors (partly buried in the floor) that are seen while exiting date back to the 2nd century B.C. and were brought from Tarsus, probably from a pagan temple. In the courtyard of the museum are some structures of Turkish origin, built at different times. These are the tombs of Sultans, a school, a clock-setting house and an ablution fountain. The minarets on the eastern side were added on to the building in the 15th century and those in the west in the 16th century.

The suppliments in Hagia Sophia made during the Ottoman Period.

THE YEREBATAN CISTERN (THE BASILICA CISTERN)

The largest and the most magnificent covered cistern in Istanbul is entered through a small building to the west of Hagia Sophia Square. The ceiling of this forest of columns is made of brick and is cross-vaulted. A street runs above a section of the cistern. Due to a basilica once situated on the cistern, it is known as the Basilica Cistern. It was built in the 6th century, in the reign of Justinian, to supply water to the palace complex nearby.

There are twenty eight columns in each of the twelve rows of columns (a total of

Two interior views of the Basilica Cistern.

336), and the cistern measures 140 metres by 70 metres. Some of the columns have plain but most of them have Corinthian capitals. The water level in the cistern changes from season to season. There are pipes at different levels in the eastern wall and water used to be distributed through these pipes. The traces left by different levels of water can be seen on the columns.

During the restoration project initiated in 1984, the floor of the cistern was scraped, and when the two metres-deep mud was removed, the original brick pavement was brought to light. Also, two Medusa heads which serve as the bases of two of the columns were discovered.

The Medusa head in the Basilica Cistern.

ISTANBUL ARCHAEOLOGICAL MUSEUMS

Istanbul Archaeological Museums is a complex of three museums: the Museum of Oriental Antiquites, the Archaeological Museum and the Tiled Pavilion Museum. The complex is located in the gardens in the first court of the Topkapı Palace. There are sixtythousand archaeological treasures, sevenhundred-sixty thousand coins and medallions, and seventy-five thousand clay tablets in these three museums.

The Archaeological Museum

The Archaeological Museum was founded by the famous painter, archaeologist and curator of the time, Osman Hamdi, and opened to the public on June 13, 1891 under the name Müze-i Hümayun (the Imperial Museum). The museum, which was rearranged and enlarged by the addition of a new wing to the building, was reopened to the public on its centannial. The gate of this majestic building designed by architect Valaury is monumental.

In the halls to the right of the entrance, examples of "Antique Age Sculpture" are exhibited. Unique examples of sculpture from the Archaic age until the end of Roman era are exhibited in the halls of "Antique Grave Stones and Reliefs", "Treasures from Persian Reign in Anatolia", "Kenan Erim Hall (Aphrodisias Relics)", "Three Marble Cities in Anatolia" (Ephesus, Miletus, Aphrodisias), "Hellenistic Sculpture", "Magnesia AD Meandrum and Tralles (Aydın) Statue Groups", "Hellenistic and Hellenistic Influenced Roman Sculpture", "Roman Art of Portrait Making", "Roman Empire Sculpture". The majority of these

The Archaeological Museum,

Statue of an Ephebe.

Statue of the River God .

artifacts was discovered during the excavations of the ancient cities in Anatolia.

Following the counters, where souvenirs and books are sold, on the left of the entrances, is the hall dedicated to Osman Hamdi, the founder of the museum. Right after this hall, treasures unearthed during the excavation of the Royal Cemetery in Sidon are exhibited. Excavation of the Cemetery was carried on by Osman Hamdi, himself.

The first of the three sarcophagi standing side by side belongs to Tabnit, the king of Sidon. A unique Lician sarcophagus and a Satrap sarcophagus are also found in this hall. Next comes the world famous Sarcophagus of Alexander the Great and the Sarcophagus of the Mourning Women. Both of these were discovered during the excavation of the Royal Cemetery in Sidon and they date back to the 4th century B.C..

Various architectural fragments are displayed in the annex building. In its ground level is the hall of "Antique Age Anatolian Architecture" and in the first storey is the hall of "Istanbul Through the Centuries". On the second storey, small archaeological finds belonging to the Paleolithic age, Early, Middle and Late Bronze ages and the Frigian State age in Anatolia are displayed under the heading "Anatolia Through the Centuries and Troy". A section of this hall is reserved for the artifacts found in Troy and the treasures discovered in the settlements I-IX are displayed in separate showcases.

On the third storey, under the heading of treasures discovered in Cyprus, Palestine and Syria are displayed in chronological order.

Hall of Hellenistic Sculpture.

Statue of Artemis.

Hall of the Roman Sculpture.

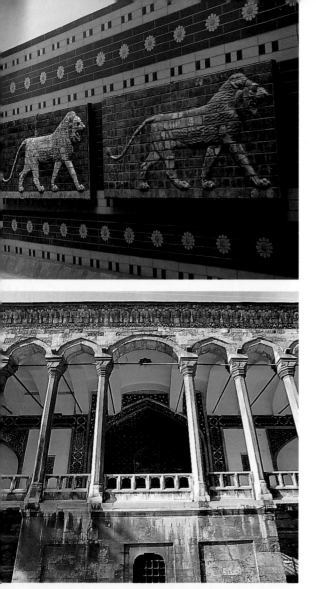

The Museum of Oriental Antiquities

The building housing the museum was constructed in 1883 to house the Academy of Fine Arts. In 1974, it was turned into a museum to exhibit the treasures of Egyptian, Mesopotamian, Arab and early Anatolian civilizations. Archives of Clay Tablets bearing cuneiform script occupies the ground floor. With its approximately seventy-five thousand pieces, the collection ranks second in the world after the British museum.

The Tiled Pavilion

It is the first pavilion built in the Topkapı Palace complex by Mehmed, the Conqueror, in 1472. Its facade, decorated with columns and arches, and the decorations of its antechamber and tiled walls are typical examples of Seljouk influenced early Ottoman architecture.

The antechamber is decorated with a long inscription created by multicoloured, cut tiles.

Vaulted rooms surround the domed interior chamber. 12th to 19th century Seljouk and Ottoman tiles and ceramics are displayed in the rooms in chronological order.

Beautiful tiles from the famous 16th century Iznik workshops constitute one of the most important sections of the museum.

Lion Relief, Babylon.

The Tiled Pavilion.

Hall of Anatolia Through the Centuries and.

Sarcophagus of Alexander the Great (Above).

Sarcophagus of Mourning Women.

THE OTTOMAN EMPIRE (1299-1922)

Central Asia was the homeland of the Turks. Over the centuries, they either migrated in large groups or organized military expeditions to various regions in Asia and even to Central Europe. Early in the 7th century, these nomadic Turkish tribes started to settle and establish states. The most important one was the small Ottoman Principality in Asia Minor which grew into the powerful Ottoman Empire that lasted for six hundred years. Although the Ottomans constituted the minority in the lands they conquered, due to their superior ability to organize and administrate efficiently, they governed these lands peaceful life for their subjects (Jews, Christians and Moslems) regard-

OTTOMAN EMPIRE
(1299 - 1922)

14 th Century: After foundation.   17 th Century: At its peak.

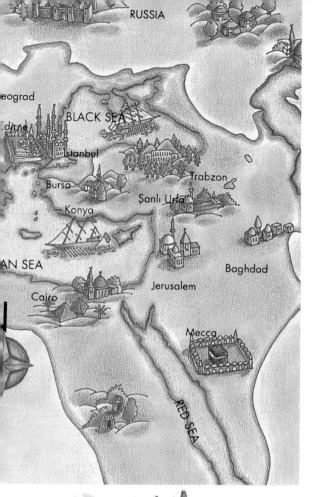

less of race, religion, culture and nationality. For almost four hundred years, the Ottoman Empire ruled the lands extending from the Arabian peninsula to Russia, from Persia to the Balkans, Greece and as far as Vienna. Towards the end of the 19th century, different nations under Ottoman rule, agitated by froeign powers, started to revolt, thereby weakening the internal structure of the empire. World War I was the final blow that brought on the collaps of the Ottoman Empire along with its allies. The lands of the empire were divided among the victors, but Kemal Atatürk led the Turkish nation to victory after a war for independence, and established the foundation of the Republic of Turkey on the remains of the Ottoman Empire, in 1923.

An aerial view of the Topkapı Palace.

Sultan II. Mahmud (above). Two Ottoman Miniatures.

THE TOPKAPI PALACE

The oldest and the largest of the remaining palaces in the world is the Topkapı Palace, a museum since 1924. The palace is located where the acropolis of Byzantium once stood on the peninsula overlooking the Golden Horn, the Bosphorus and the Sea of Marmara. The palace complex covers an area of 700,000 sqm. and it is surrounded by five kilometres of walls.

The Topkapı Palace is the second palace built by Turks in Istanbul. After young Sultan Mehmed II conquered the city in 1453 he had his first palace built at the site where the Istanbul University stands today. Soon afterward he ordered a new palace and in 1479, after 14 years, the Topkapı Palace (initially called the New Palace) was ready for occupancy as the Sultan's residence and centre of government.

The Topkapı Palace is typical of Turkish palaces. The distinctive element of its plan is a series of open courtyards with trees to provide shade. Each courtyards is for a functions and they connected to one another by monumental doors. Functional buildings are arranged on the sides of courtyards. The palace plan today is not the same as when it was built, since Sultans succeeding Mehmed the Conqueror have made additions and annexes.

In 1853 when the new and ostentatious Dolmabahçe Palace was completed, the Topkapı Palace lost its status as the official palace and fell into oblivion. It was only after the Republic was founded that the Topkapı Palace was cared for. The repair work that went on for more than fifty years finally restored the Topkapı Palace to its original inconspicuous beauty. Today, it is used as a museum to exhibit works of art and many priceless artifacts. It is a museum with few rivals.

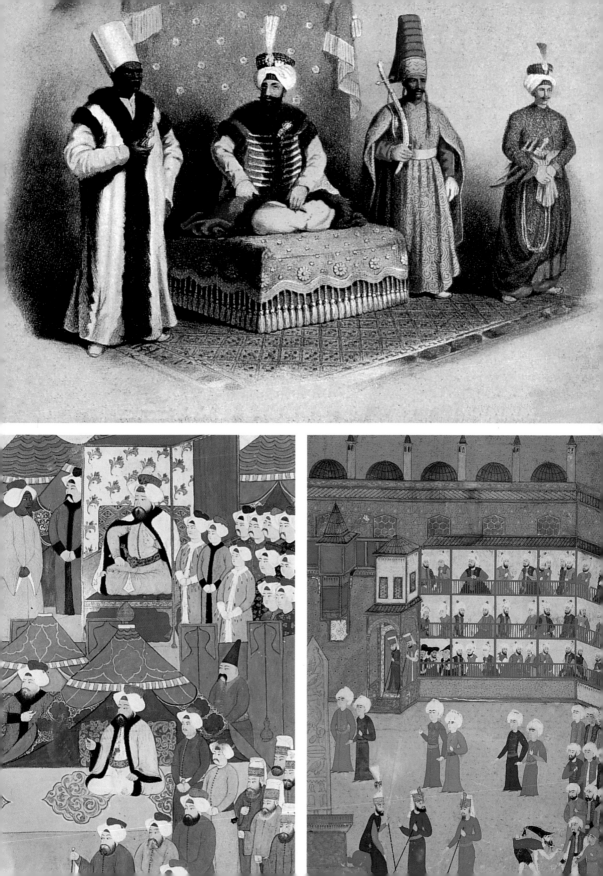

Plan of the Topkapı Palace

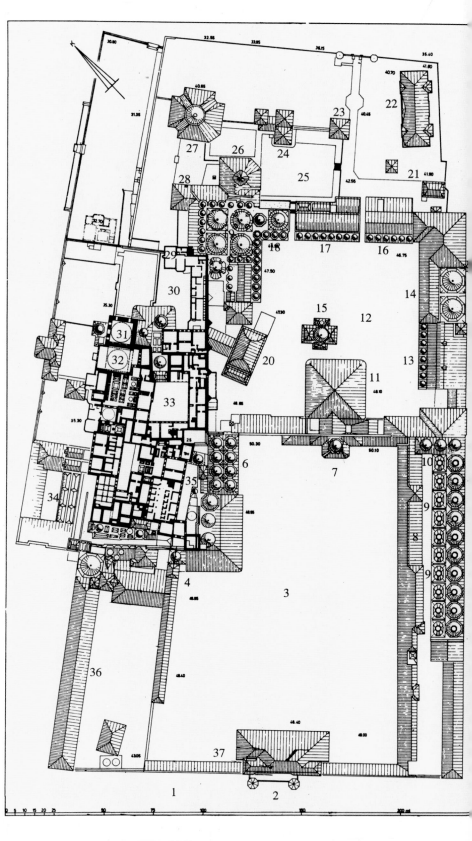

The Gate of Felicity: the third gate of the Topkapı Palace.

The functions of the Topkapı Palace while it was used as the official palace of Ottoman Sultans were quite different from those of most other palaces. Although it was primarily the residence of the incumbent sultan, it also oserved as the headquarters of the government where the cabinet of ministers met. It also housed the state mint and the archives, as well as the highest institution of education of the realm, the university of the sultan and the state. In other words, the palace was virtually the heart, the brain, the very centre of the Ottoman Empire. It was long after the construction of the palace that the Harem quarters were added to it. The Ottoman Empire was the largest and longest-lived of the sixteen sovereign empires Turks have founded at various times. The giant empire that lasted for 622 years kept many countries along the shores of the Mediterranean and the Black Sea under its benevolent reign, merging many peoples of different races and religions. The only other empire in history ever to have kept such a vast realm for such a long time was the Roman Empire. During the course of the Ottoman Empire, 36 sultans occupied the throne, and those reigning from the 16th century onwards also bore the title of Caliph, the religious head of Islam.

Life in the Topkapı Palace started at dawn and continued throughout the day with ceremonies and strict rules of protocol governing every possible situation and event. Everybody was obliged to abide by the customs and traditions of the Palace that had developed over centuries. Even during the decline of the Empire, the rules never slackened. The protocol rules of the western world were highly influenced by those dominant in the Topkapı Palace.

The seaside mansions and pavillions of the Topkapı Palace were destroyed by the end of the 19th century.

Visiting the Palace: The First Court

The first and outermost court of the Palace is entered through the Bab-ı Hümayun (Imperial Gate). The monumental fountain outside the gate is a precious example of 18th century Turkish art. Surrounding the first court are the palace bakery, mint, palace quarters and stores for firewood. On the terraces below were the vegetable gardens that supplied the palace. Çinili Köşk (The Tiled Lodge), the first building built in the Topkapı Palace complex, is also inside this court. Immediately upon entering the court, one sees the Hagia Eirene; a Byzantine church-turned-museum dating back to the 6th century.

The Second Court

The actual entrance to the Topkapı Palace Museum is the second gate called Bab-ı Selam (Gate of Salutation), through which one enters the second court that was reserved for the administrative functions of the state. To this court, only representatives of the Janissaries on paydays were admitted. Certain state ceremonies were held here. Historians have noted that during such ceremonies which were attended by as many as five or even ten thousand people, absolute silence prevailed. For ceremonies the Sultan himself attended, the imperial throne was placed in front of the gate at the other end of the court and all those present stood facing him with their hands clasped in gesture of reverence. To the left of the court was the administrative section where the cabinet met. The only tower in the palace grounds is called the Tower of Justice because justice in the name of the state was dispensed from these quarters. The tower was also used to watch the whole city and the port, and the only entrance to it is through the Harem.

Left: Topkapı Palace, 1st Courtyard (16th century).

An Ottoman armour and helmet (15th century).

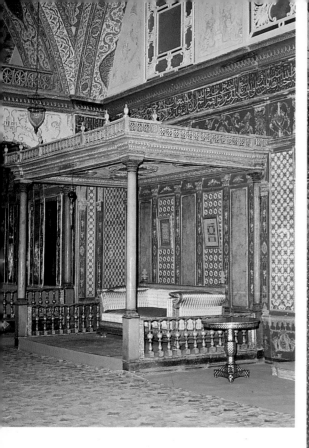

The Harem: The Imperial Hall.

The Harem

The Harem section of the Topkapı Palace is made up of about 400 rooms scattered around small inner courts. Throughout the history of the palace, the Harem quarters underwent alterations continuously. It was the private quarters of the Sultan's residence where his mother, brothers and sisters, wives, children and other members of the family, as well as the servants and eunuchs lived. Throughout the centuries, many stories have been told about these private quarters of the palace, entrance to which was strictly prohibited to outsiders. However, some of these must be regarded as myth, and the information backed by evidence points to a way of life in the Harem not as eccentric as people have been led to believe, but nevertheless interesting.

The Fruit Room, the Harem.

The concubines (*cariye*) to serve the Sultan and his family were hand-picked from the most beautiful and healthy young maidens of various races or were given to the Sultan as gifts. These girls, who were admitted to the Harem at an age barely out of childhood, were trained for years under the strictest discipline. After becoming perfectly familiar with the rules and customs of the palace, they were allowed to serve the Sultan. Some of these girls were able to attract the attention of the Sultan and hence his favours, and occasionally even to become wives. In the Ottoman Empire there was no status as an Empress. The power to run the Harem was vested in the Sultan's mother. In this setting of wealth and splendor, gossip, rivalry and struggle to get closer to the Sultan were parts of daily life. When a Sultan died or was forced to abdicate and a new one assumed the throne, the harem of the former was moved to another palace. During the reign of a Sultan with a weak personality and little authority, the Harem would often emerge as a political power and indulge in power-play and intrigue.

Today, only a part of the Harem section is open as a museum. While touring these empty rooms and the gloomy corridors, the visitor needs to work his imagination exhaustively to visualize the Harem as it was in its heyday.

The Kitchen and the Porcelains Section

On the right side of the second court one can see the palace kitchen with its twenty tall chimneys. In the days when the palace was living, more than 1,000 assistant cooks worked in the kitchen, preparing the menus for the different parts of the palace. A part of the kitchen has been kept in its original

The Hall with a heath and the reading room of Ahmed III. The Harem.

A dragon-shaped pitcher and a cobalt blue pitcher two blue - white plates (14th century).

Left: Akağalar Gate (above), the Arz Odası.

The Library of Ahmed III.

state, and the rest has been converted into a museum where porcelains and china are exhibited. About 2,500 of the 12,000-plus pieces of chinaware of Chinese and Japanese origin in the palace collection is on display here. Furthermore, selected pieces of porcelains and glassware made in Istanbul are exhibited in chronological order. Recently this section of the Topkapı Palace Museum has been rearranged to include also European porcelains and silverware from the palace collection.

The Third Court

The entrance to the third court of the Topkapı Palace, the private court of the Sultans, is through the gate called Bâbü's-sa'âde (Gate of Felicity). Nobody without special permission could pass through that gate, and those with permission were admitted, only in the company of white eunuchs, to the Sultan's private court. Surrounding

this court were the Palace University, the throne chamber, the Sultan's treasury and the sanctuary of Holy Islamic relics. The Sultan met with the ambassadors of foreign countries and the high officials of his government in the throne chamber that is located directly opposite the gate. The servants to the throne chamber were specially picked from deaf-mutes for obvious security reasons. Also, certain officers of the Ottoman Army who were also prominent faculty members of the palace school served the Sultans.

The Library of Ahmed III located at the centre of the court is a perfect example of the blend of the baroque style with Turkish architecture.

The school in the Sultan's private courtyard trained candidates for positions of responsibility in government. The graduates of the school served locally and usually successfully in the administration and organi-

65

Two different sultans caftans.

zation of the vast empire. Most of the Viziers and Grand Viziers of the government graduated from this school.

The Imperial Costumes Section

There is no exhibition in the world that can compare to the Imperial Costumes Section of the Topkapı Palace Museum. The costumes made of fabric woven on the palace looms and ornamented with gold and silver braids have been carefully preserved since the 15th century and are in excess of 2,500 in number. Also exhibited in the same section are silk prayer rugs, masterpieces of Turkish art, that were used by the Sultans.

The Treasury

The Treasury section of the Topkapı Palace Museum is the richest collection of its kind in the world. All the pieces exhibited

in the four halls are authentic origina Masterpieces of Turkish craftsmen fr different centuries and priceless creatic from the Far East, India and Europe fas nate the visitors. In each of the four roo there is an imperial throne used in a diff ent period of the empire. Ceremonial att and accessories, weapons, water pip Turkish coffee cups and other vess adorned with gold and precious stones the main items in the first room. The sec room is known as the "emeralds and ot precious stones". Huge uncut emera weighing a few kilograms each and Topkapı dagger with four large emeralds the hilt and embellished with diamonds t has become the symbol of the palace is s in this room. In the third room, enemal pieces, medals and decorations given to sultans by foreign countries, the twin sc gold candelabra each weighing 48 ki grams, and the most renowned throne in

The Topkapı Dagger.

The Spoonseller's Diamond.

palace -the golden throne used on the coronation day of the Sultans- are displayed. Connecting the third and fourth rooms is a balcony which commands a magnificient view of the entrance of the Bosphorus and the Asiatic coast. In the fourth room are the grand throne of Turko-Indian origin and many pieces adorned with precious stones which fascinate every visitor. In addition to the four rooms, there is also a very rich collection of watches, and table and wall clocks in a room across the treasury in the third court.

The Holy Relics of Islam, which used to belong to the Prophet Mohammed are kept and exhibited in a special sanctuary by the third courty, and in an adjoining hall a collection illustrating the consummate skill of Turkish calligraphers is exhibited.

The Topkapı Dagger: The dagger that has become the symbol of the palace and the treasury is an invaluable product of 18th

century Turkish craftsmanship. There are four large emeralds on the hilt, the one on the top concealing a watch.

The Kaşıkçı Diamond: The pear-shaped 86-carat Kaşıkçı Diamond is among the largest in the world. Its origin is not known. Legend attributes its name (the Spoonmaker's -or Spoonseller's Diamond) to its sale by a pauper, who was unaware of its value, to a merchant in return for a few wooden spoons. However, the consensus of the experts is that the Kaşıkçı Diamond is in fact the "Pigot" Diamond named after an officer in the French army who is known to have bought a diamond of similar dimensions and shape in India in 1774. The Pigot Diamond could be traced, after numerous owners, to Napoleon Bonaparte's mother and then to an Ottoman governor. Since the Kaşıkçı Diamond was transferred to the Ottoman treasury among the treasure of governor Tepedelenli Ali Paşa, who was exe-

67

The Nadir Shah Throne.

cuted in the 1840's after conviction for rebellion against the state, it is highly probable that the Kaşıkçı and Pigot diamonds are the same.

The beautiful, specially cut Kaşıkçı Diamond is surrounded by 49 smaller pieces of diamond embedded in gold in two rows.

The Throne: This throne, made and presented to Sultan Mahmud I in the 18th century, is a masterpiece of Turko-Indian art. It is actually a portable throne dismountable into 223 pieces. The most outstanding feature of the throne, even surpassing the multitude of emeralds, rubies and pearls used to form the motifs of spring flowers, is the excellence of the gold inlay and enamel work rated by some as the ultimate in these tech-

A cremonial Helmet. (16th century).

Above, right: A jewelled glass bowl, A glass pitcher.

Below, right: Two Ceremonial Canteens (16th century).

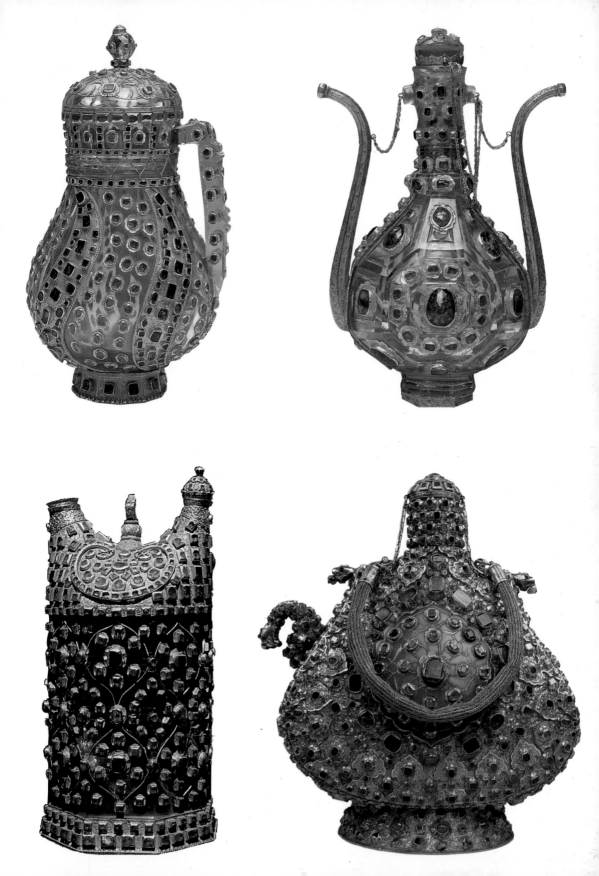

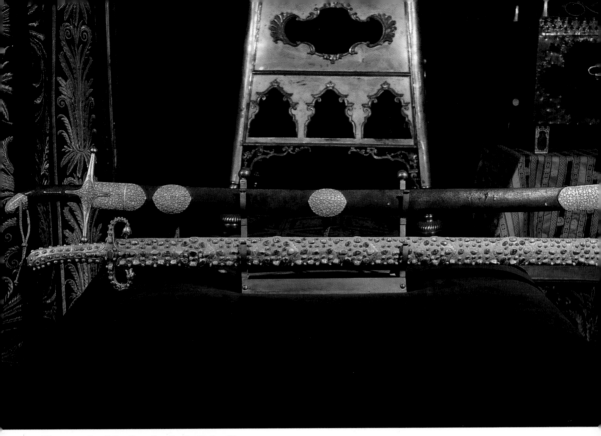

The swords of the Prophet in the Privy Room.

niques. Now the largest item being exhibited in the fourth room of the Topkapı Palace Treasury, the throne has a footstool and a beautifully embroidered cushion as accessories.

The Holy Relics of Islam

The Holy Relics of Islam brought from Egypt early in the 16th century after the capture of that land by the Ottoman Empire have since then been kept inside a sanctuary in the Topkapı Palace.

The conquest of Egypt had passed the title of Caliph to the Ottoman Sultans, thus increasing the power of the Ottoman throne. The Holy Relics that served in part as the symbols of Ottoman power include personal articles and garments of the Prophet Mohammed, one of the oldest manuscript copies of the Koran and the keys to Kaaba. Apart from their religious significance, all these items also are prominent works of art.

The Fourth Court

Passageways connect the third court to the fourth where there are pavilions surrounded by gardens. The only wooden pavilions in the palace, the Baghdad and Revan Pavilions and the Mecidiye Pavilion, the last structure built in the Topkapı Palace complex, are found in this court. The terrace by the Baghdad Pavilion is the best place to enjoy the magnificent panorama of the Golden Horn and across it, the Galata Section of the city, as well as the unique skyline of Istanbul with its domes and minarets.

At the edge of the terrace there is a gold plated bronze canopy, and next to it is the Circumcision Room which has tile panels decorating the wall by the entrance.

A view of the Baghdad Pavilion.

The Mustafa Paşa Pavilion.

The Constantinos Column (Çemberlitaş).

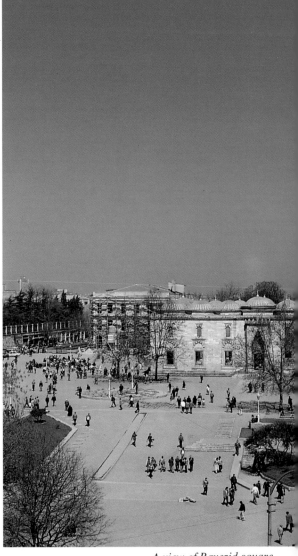

A view of Bayezid square.

ÇEMBERLİTAŞ

It was erected to honour Constantine the Great, in the centre of an oval-shaped square on the second hill of Istanbul, and on the occasion of the dedication of Istanbul as the new capital of the Roman Empire in 330 A.D.. The oval-shaped square, known as the Forum Constantine, was surrounded by columned porticos. Çemberlitaş is also known as the Hooped or Burnt Column. It stood taller than it does today, and a gilded statue of Constantine the Great, posing as the sun god, stood on it. The porphyry blocks of the column, which had cracked in time and survived a fire, were reinforced with iron hoops.

The white marble capital was placed on it in the 12th century, and the stone wall seen in the lower section was built in the 18th century to reinforce the column. It was believed that relics dating back to early Christianity used to be kept in the small chamber under the column. The course of the avenue that passes by the column has not changed since Constantine the Great.

The Bayezid Tower.

BAYEZID SQUARE

It was built in 393 during the reign of Theodosius I, as the largest square in the city. A gigantic victory arch used to stand in the middle of the square which was called the Bull's Square (Forum Tauri) because of the large bronze bull's head there.

There was a bronze statue of the emperor on the arch. Today, only a few marble blocks remain of the arch itself, but nothing remains of the monumental fountains which were to the north of the square. They used to be the largest fountains in the city then, and the Aqueduct of Valens used to supply water to them. The buildings of the University of Istanbul occupy the large courtyard on the grounds where the Conqueror had built a palace. The monumental gate and the tallest tower in the city, the Bayezid fire-lookout tower, which stands in the gardens of the University, were built in the 19th century. The Bayezid Mosque and its complex (school and baths) are the main buildings around the square.

73

THE COVERED BAZAAR
(The Grand Bazaar)

The oldest and the largest covered market place in the world is situated in the centre of the city. Resembling a giant labyrinth, it consists of approximately sixty lanes and more than three-thousand shops. This unique and interesting market place is one of those places in the city which one must see to really appreciate.

In 1461, Mehmed the Conqueror built an area for the shops selling items necessary for the textile industry. This nucleus of today's Covered Bazaar (iç bedesten) is a rectangular area, surrounded inside and outside, by shops. The Conqueror built another area (sandal bedesteni) later, close to the "iç bedesten". There are shops only along the

Two different views of the Covered Bazaar.

Different scenes from the Covered Bazaar.

outer wall of the "sandal bedesteni". During the time of the Conqueror, there were 950 shops.

The city-like bazaar is completely covered and it grew in size over the years. In the old days, each lane was reserved for a different profession and the quality of the handicrafts produced was strictly controlled. Business practices were governed by strict traditional ethics. Valuable fabrics, jewellery weapons and antique objets used to be sold by merchants whose families, for generations, had dealt in the same trade.

The bazaar, which was first built by the Conqueror and then enlarged by Süleyman the Magnificent, was originally constructed of wood. In 1700, it suffered greatly in a fire. In 1701, it was repaired by using stone and bricks, in the shape we see today.

The bazaar survived earthquakes, and a few fires towards the end of the last century. During repairs, it has lost its original form and features, and has changed for the worse.

Today, many of the streets in the bazaar have changed character. Guilds such as the "quilt makers", "slipper makers" and "fez makers" exist only in the street names.

Jewellers line the main street in the bazaar. The goldsmiths are on a side street at right angles to the main street. Prices vary, and bargaining is customary in these rather small stores. The Covered Bazaar still retains its old charm and is an attractive sight to see, but since 1970, modern and spacious shops have been built near the main entrance to shop in comfort. The bazaar is quite crowded at any hour of the day, and the shop owners try their best to attract the attention of shoppers and lure them into their shops. The spacious stores that line the street leading to the main entrance to the bazaar sell handmade items produced in Turkey.

A "Carpet Shows" in the Bazaar 54 which has a rich carpet collection.

HANDMADE TURKISH CARPETS

The art of weaving hand-knotted carpets is the oldest handicraft of the Turks. The two richest carpet museums in the world are located in Istanbul. Today, carpets, still knotted in the old traditional ways, are produced in just about every region in Turkey. The carpets are made of pure wool, silk, or wool and cotton blends in various sizes and designs. Each carpet is a product of tradition, high quality raw materials, special techniques, patience and months long labour. Besides these, in certain centres, subsidized by the state, handmade carpets are produced like an industry.

Hereke, near Istanbul, is the most famous centre of handmade silk carpet production. The carpets made here, in Konya and in Kayseri are the most sought after carpets.

SHOPPING IN ISTANBUL

The Grand Bazaar of Istanbul, with its thousands of shops is a famous and unique shopping centre. BAZAAR 54, the leading establishment in the Grand Bazaar, offers fully washed, top quality handmade carpets selected by experts. The old and new carpet collections of Bazaar 54, containing thousands of items of top quality Turkish workmanship, are Istanbul's largest and richest. Bazaar 54 is an authorized exporter with a worldwide shipping service. Besides carpets, its handmade, fully guaranteed jewellery collection is also worth seeing.

Above, left: Girls weaving carpets. Below: Carpet Show in Bazaar 54. The jewellery section in Bazaar 54.

The Süleymaniye Mosque.

THE SÜLEYMANİYE MOSQUE

A beauty outstanding even among all those domes and minarets that define the skyline of Istanbul, the Süleymaniye Mosque is the largest and most grandiose in the city. It facinates every visitor with the aesthetic supremacy of its interior and exterior, and its harmonious and pleasant proportions. By all standards, the Süleymaniye Mosque is an architectural masterpiece.

In the 16th century, the Ottoman Empire was at its peak and the zenith of the century is the forty-seven year reign (the longest ever in the Ottoman Empire) of Sultan Süleyman the Magnificient. The great Sultan had recruited the famous Turkish architect Sinan to plan and build a mosque bearing his own name. Sinan, a genius of the world of architecture and the founder/benefactor of the Turkish classical school of ar-

chitecture, completed the huge mosque complex that also included schools, a library, a Turkish bath, a public kitchen, a caravanserai, a hospital and shops. It was built between the years 1550 and 1557, thus proving that he indeed deserved the title of "Great" that was granted to him.

One has to stand at a distance to appreciate fully the exterior beauty of the Süleymaniye Mosque. The best site for this is the Galata coast of the Golden Horn, especially the Galata Tower.

The nave of the four-minaret imperial mosque is covered by a huge dome. The main entrance to the mosque is reached by passing through an inner courtyard with a symbolic ablution fountain at the centre and porticoes on all four sides.

The spaciousness and unity of the nave of the mosque and the rather subtle decoration of the interior walls all contribute to an aura of dignified grandeur. The central cu-

The Interior of Süleymaniye Mosque.   *The Süleymaniye Mosque.*

pola, 53 m. high at the keystone and 26.50 m. in diameter is supported by four pendentives on four pillars. All the architectural elements constituting the dome are in proper harmony. The static balance, too, is perfect. The numerous earthquakes that shook the city of Istanbul since the 16th century did not cause even a single crack. The inner surface of the dome is decorated with baroque painting from the 19th century. The handmade carpet on the floor of the nave is new having been given to the mosque in the 1960's.

The most eye-catching element of the interior decor is the original stained-glass windows of Turkish motifs on the wall of the mihrab (prayer niche). The incospicuous little chanter's balcony is at the front of pulpit. The walls around the minber (pulpit) near the mihrab are decorated with beautiful ceramic tiles.

The Sultan's Box is to the left of the mihrab. The walls of the mosque adorned with verses from the Koran are regarded as ultimate in the Turkish art of calligraphy. Along the walls of the mosque, with the exception of the southern wall, there are balconies for women.

The brass grill to the right of the entrance is a typical example of 18th century craftsmanship. In the forecourt of the mosque, the tombs of Sultan Süleyman and Roxelana, his favourite wife, lie side by side.

And at one corner of the Süleymaniye Complex, there is a small and humble grave where rests Sinan the Great, the grandmaster of Turkish architecture who spent fifty years of his ninety-nine years as the chief architect of a powerful empire.

THE VALİDE SULTAN MOSQUE (Yeni Cami)

It was the last imperial mosque built in the classical style. It was built next to the pier in Eminönü Harbour which was a very busy district then as well. Due to the heavy traffic on Galata Bridge and the heavy sea-traffic created by the boats docking at the piers in front of it, the mosque is seen by thousands of people every day.

Its construction was started by Safiye Sultan, mother of Sultan Mehmed III, in 1589, but it was interrupted in 1603 upon the death of the Sultan. Its architect was Da-vut Ağa, a student of Sinan. The construction was resumed in 1661 by Turhan Sultan, mother of the Sultan, Mehmet IV. and was

Above: The Valide Sultan Mosque (Yeni Cami).
The Egyptian Bazaar.

completed in 1664. Only the large covered bazaar, the mausoleums and the magnificent fountain of the mosque's scattered complex have survived.

Between the southern side of the mosque and the "L" shaped Spice Bazaar is the Flower Market. The tea houses here are always full of people resting. The Spice Bazaar is the second largest covered market place in the city.

The steamships, which had docked for fifty years in front of the mosque, have been taken out of service, and the minarets and the facades which had been blackened by soot have been cleaned.

Above: The Spice Bazaar (Egyptian Bazaar).
Left: Flower Bazaar, Eminönü.

The Galata Bridge.

THE GOLDEN HORN (HALİÇ)

The Golden Horn, which is a natural harbour, played an important role in the development of the city of Istanbul. It is a narrow inlet dividing the European side into two. Opposite the ancient city is the Galata district. The Golden Horn is approximately 8 km. long and its entrance from the Bosphorus is quite wide. Two streams drain into this inlet at its deep end. There are no tides or currents in this unusually safe harbour which has been used since the establishment of the city. Due to the fertile lands around it, the great variety of fish in its waters, the two streams draining into it and its shape, it was referred to as the Golden (meaning fertile) Horn. There are three bridges on the Golden Horn. The oldest

A festival day in the Golden Horn.

The Golden Horn shores.

one, the Galata Bridge has been replaced by a new bridge which was opened to traffic in 1992. During the Byzantine Empire a thick chain used to be stretched across its entrance to keep enemy fleets out of the Golden Horn. Today, there is heavy traffic in the vicinity of Galata Bridge, which was built at the entrance to the Golden Horn. Ferry boats serving the Islands and the districts along the Asian shores, and the big cruise ships that bring tourists use the docks in the area.

The shipyards and the Sepetçiler (Basket Weavers) Pavilion (serving as headquarters of International Press Agencies) of Topkapı Palace, the railway station built in 1890, which is the last stop for trains arriving from Europe, the Valide Sultan Mosque and the Spice Bazaar line the shore at the entrance to the Golden Horn.

Galata Bridge and its vicinity is the most dynamic and colourful part of the city. Dur-

ing all hours of the day, there is heavy traffic of cars and pedestrians on the bridge which offers a magnificent view of the old city of Istanbul.

In the 1950's, many shipyards, factories, and other businesses were established along the shores of the Golden Horn and they contributed heavily to the pollution of its waters and the deterioration of the once scenic area. Since 1983, pollution has been controlled and the area has started to recover. In the last few years, more than four thousand houses, businesses and factories along its shores have been torn down and replaced by parks.

There is an interesting church on the shore along the edge of the historic city. Its mouldings and steel parts were made in Vienna, brought here and mounted on the building. This buildings is part of the Bulgarian Church. Further down is the Orthodox Patriarchate in the Fener district located amid the remains of the city walls and old districts. Across Fener, in the Kasımpaşa district, there is a big 19th century pavilion which, today, is the Navy Headquarters.

THE EYÜP SULTAN MOSQUE

Eyüp is considered a sacred site by Moslems. Eyüp-el-Ensari, the flag bearer of Mohammed, was killed here in the 7th century during the Arab seige. His grave, discovered during the conquest of Istanbul, was enclosed by a large mausoleum, and next to it the first prominent mosque in Istanbul was built.

The original mosque, built by the Conqueror, collapsed in an earthquake in the 18th century and was replaced by another mosque completed in 1800. On holy days of Islam and every Friday, the mausoleum of Eyüp is visited by throngs of believers. The centuries-old trees, flocks of pigeons flying and believers praying, create a lively and mystic atmosphere in the environs of the mosque and the mausoleums.

After the Conqueror, each succeeding sultan completed his coronation and sword-bearing ceremonies by visiting the Eyüp Sultan district. The hills and slopes behind the district are occupied by cemeteries.

The famous Pierre Loti Café is on the first hill behind the Eyüp district. The famous French poet-author Pierre Loti who loved Istanbul, came here quite often to admire the view of the Golden Horn.

Right: The Eyüp Sultan Mosque.

Above: The prayers at the Eyüp Sultan Mosque.

Below: Two views from Pierre Loti Café.

KARİYE MUSEUM (THE CHURCH OF ST. SAVIOUR IN CHORA MONASTERY)

The word chora means "outside the city, the countryside". Probably a small church which had been built here before the 5th century Roman city walls gave its name to the other churches built later at the same site. The existing edifice is dated to the 11th-14th centuries. besides its attractive exterior, the mosaics and frescoes inside are masterpieces of "the Renaissance" of Byzantine art. These decorations and the additions built in the 14th century were ordered by Theodore Metochites. The mosaic panels in the two narthexes upon entering depict scenes from the lives of the Virgin and Christ (as described in the Bible). Frescoes depicting religious themes are in the side chapel. Figures of the members of the palace and the church are seen among them. When the church was converted into a mosque in the beginning of the 16th century, the mosaics and frescoes were covered by whitewash. Starting in 1950, these have been restored and cleaned by the Byzantine Institute of the U.S.A..

The Chora monastery and its church became neighbours with the Imperial Palaces and acquired importance in time. Master craftsmen decorated the building with great care under the difficult conditions present in the 14th century.

The famous scholar and state dignitary of the time, Theodore Metochites, built the side chapel, which was completed in 1320, and the exonarthex. The mosaics and frescoes were also completed during his time. The mosaic panels were created by a group of artisans. The mosaics on the upper sections of the nave have not survived.

Left: The Kariye Museum.

Above Right: The geneology of Christ (detail)

Below: Virgin Mary and the Christ child.

Ἡ ἈΝΆϹΤΑϹΙϹ

In Byzantine art, the name or the monogram of the personality depicted used to be inscribed next to the figure.

The vicinity of Kariye Museum which resembles a picture gallery, has been altered in recent times. Some old houses have been restored and turned into cafés and pensions.

Pages 90-91: Jesus Saving the Souls of Adam and Eve, a fresco.

The presentation of Mary to Bishop Zacharias (above).

An interior view of the Kariye Museum (below).

A Turkish belly dancer (right).

GALATA AND BEYOĞLU DISTRICTS

The Galata district is situated in an area that commands a view of the entrance to the Golden Horn and the harbour. During the Byzantine and Ottoman eras, the district was settled first by the Venetians and then, beginning in the 14th century, by the Genoese. Latin merchants used to control commerce in the Galata district where, in the 14th and 15th centuries, a tall lookout-tower and city walls were built. Many of the streets in the district are lined with eighty and ninety year old houses, and Galata resembles the cities along the Mediterranean coast in that age.

For many years, people moving into Istanbul from different parts of Anatolia have settled in this district. Many of the churches and synagogues as well as the German, Austrian and Greek schools still function.

The Galata Tower.

Çiçek Pasajı, Beyoğlu.

The Istiklal Avenue, Beyoğlu.

GALATA TOWER

Built on the hill in the Galata district, it was used as a lookout-tower in the 14th and 15th centuries. Located at a site overlooking the harbour and the entrance to the Bosphorus, it commands a magnificent view of the historic city. The upper sections of the tower were constructed in the Turkish era when it was used as a fire-watch tower. Its conical cap was restored to its original early 19th century appearance in 1969. A restaurant and a night club occupy the upper two storeys, and a balcony surrounds the tower.

TÜNEL AND BEYOĞLU

Tünel (the underground) which connects the shores of the Golden Horn to the Beyoğlu district on the hill, is located in Karaköy Square. This second underground in Europe was opened for services in 1880 and today, it is the shortest line in the world. İstiklal Caddesi stretches on the hills in the Beyoğlu district, and starts at the upper entrance to "Tünel", and extends all the way to Taksim Square. Beginning in the 16th century, Beyoğlu became the district where foreign embassy buildings were constructed and minorities lived. Near the upper entrance to Tünel is the Galata Mevlevihanesi which is a museum today. The lodge is the most interesting of its kind. There are interesting collections of books and musical instruments in the Divan Edebiyatı (old Ottoman Poetry) Museum on the first floor of the lodge.

When Ankara became the capital after the foundation of the Turkish Republic, all the foreign embassies were moved to the new capital, and the old embassy buildings in Istanbul were converted into consulates.

İstiklal Caddesi used to be the main street famous for its elegant shops, lively

Atatürk's statue in the Taksim Square.

and colourful nightlife, theatres and cinemas, but in recent years it has deteriorated. In 1990, to improve the area, the traffic was rerouted, a tramway line was installed all along the street and the buildings were renovated. The Catholic churches seen on the side of the street overlooking the Bosphorus have held services since the last century.

TAKSİM

Halfway towards the Taksim Square is the small Galatasaray Square where the famous lycée of the same name is located. Near the square, there is a partially collapsed building known as the Flower Passage, where there are many small restaurants and beerhouses. The street running next to this passage is lined with shops selling many varieties of fish, vegetables and fruit.

Taksim Square, surrounded by the Atatürk Cultural Centre in the north and five star hotels, is considered the centre of Istanbul and the Atatürk Monument is in the centre of the square.

Cumhuriyet Caddesi stretches from the square to the Şişli district, and there are many travel agencies along this road. After the Radio House, the Officers, Club Guest House and the Military Museum, come the shops and boutiques selling clothing, shoes etc. The stores in the Osmanbey area are famous for the high quality of the products they sell.

MILITARY MUSEUM

This is one of the leading museums of its kind in the world. It occupies two large buildings located in the gardens of the Officers' Club near the Hilton Hotel. In the two-storeyed main older section, military uni-

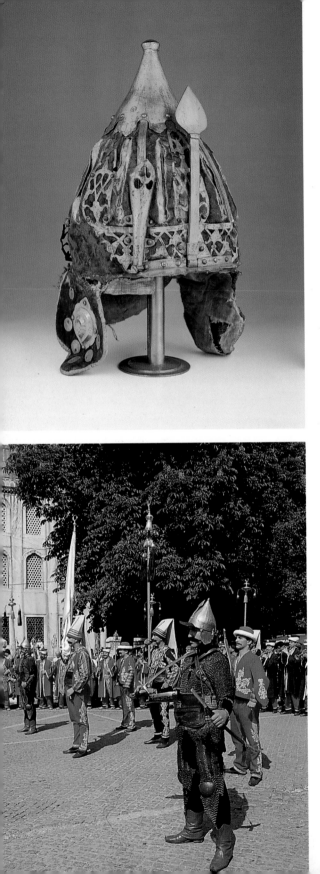

forms, weapons, and tools used in the Empire and the Republic are displayed. The new building is reserved for old tents including the imperial tents.

THE JANISSARY BAND

The official band of the ottoman army was known as the Mehter (the Janissary Band). This band of thousands of members used to lead the armies going on campaigns. The band, which had its own special way of marching, used to play stirring marches during attacks and sieges. Today, the oldest band in the world still plays its music in its own characteristic style, on certain days in the Military Museum, and during special ceremonies and concerts.

THE MUSEUM OF FINE ARTS, TURKISH PAINTING AND SCULPTURES

It occupies the fourth section, the quarters of the Crown Prince, in the Dolmabahçe Palace. The entrance to the museum and the Hareket Pavilion, which is used for special exhibits, is on the seaward side of Beşiktaş.

Works of Turkish painters from the 19th century upto today are found in the museum. There are approximately 2,500 original paintings, 250 reproductions and 400 statues in the museums which will soon be modernized. Contemporary Turkish works of art are displayed from time to time in the special sections in the museums and palaces in Istanbul, in the Atatürk Cultural Centre and in certain other art galleries.

The Military Museum: A ceremonial helmet.

The Janissary Band.

Right: Two different views of the Naval Museum.

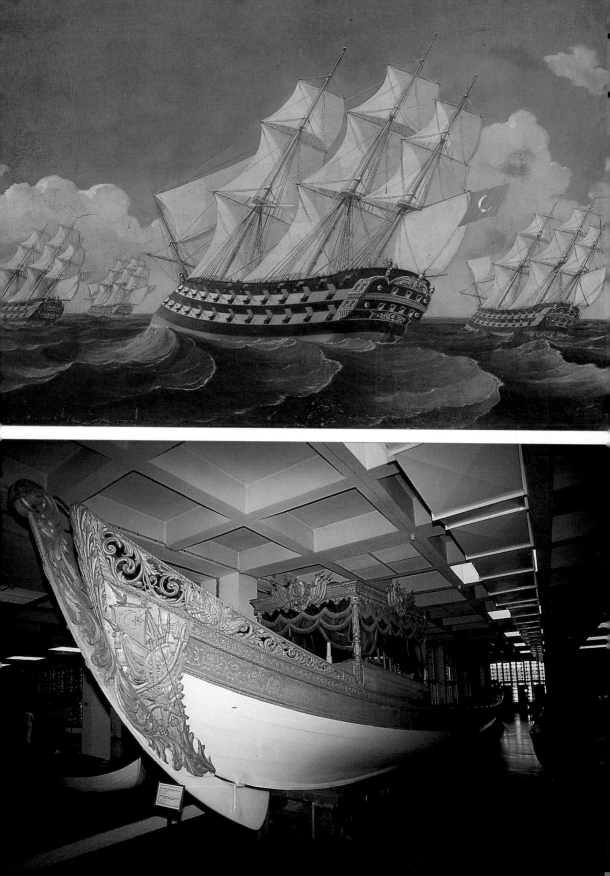

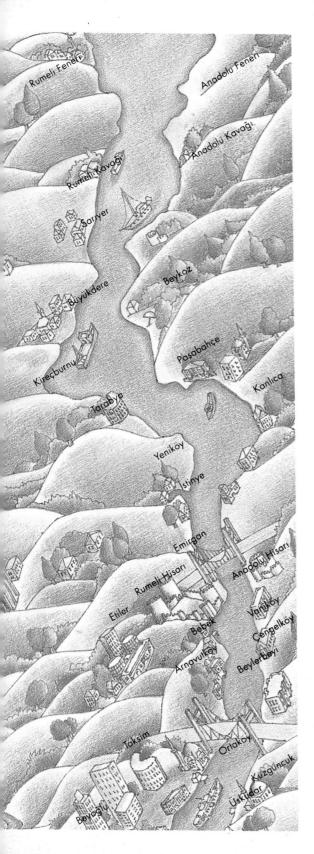

Rumeli Feneri
Anadolu Feneri
Anadolu Kavağı
Rumeli Kavağı
Sarıyer
Beykoz
Büyükdere
Paşabahçe
Kireçburnu
Kanlıca
Tarabya
Yeniköy
İstinye
Emirgan
Anadolu Hisarı
Rumeli Hisarı
Etiler
Vaniköy
Bebek
Çengelköy
Arnavutköy
Beylerbeyi
Taksim
Ortaköy
Kuzguncuk
Beyoğlu
Üsküdar

THE NAVAL MUSEUM

Situated in the Beşiktaş district along the shores of the Bosphorus, this museum is next to the park where the statue and the mausoleum of the famous 16th century Turkish Admiral Barbaros Hayreddin are located. Old boats are displayed in the main building, and along with the interesting items in the gardens, the museum has an impressive collection. The main building is three-storeyed, and models of boats, sections from Atatürk's personal yacht, tools and other items used in the decoration of old ships are displayed in the small rooms and halls of the building. Paintings depicting various naval events decorate the walls. The basement is reserved for the parts and sections of the ships which had served in the Turkish navy. There are also torpedoes on display. Behind the main building, there is another buildings entered from the sea side. It is reserved for the Old Boats Gallery. The well preserved, elegant boats of the Sultans, members of the palace and other important people of the 18th-20th centuries are displayed.

THE BOSPHORUS (BOĞAZİÇİ)

One of the most beautiful sights in the world, the Bosphorus, is a strait that runs a winding course between the two continents from one sea to another. It is a natural border between Europe and Asia and it is the only outlet of the Black Sea which is connected to the Aegean through the Bosphorus and the Dardanelles.

With old seaside mansions, mosques, palaces, restaurants and beaches along its shores, the Bosphorus resembles a wide river. Woods and residences cover the hills rising behind its shores. It looks magnificent

A panoromic view from Ortaköy.

A typical scenery from the Bosphorus shores.

The Leander's Tower.

in every season and is especially beautiful in the spring when it is adorned with the pink flowers of Judas-trees. The Bosphorus is unforgettable.

Two fortresses, constructed halfway up the Bosphorus on opposite shores, stand facing each other. These, built by the Turks, and the other earlier fortresses on the hills near the Black Sea, are military installations indicating the strategic importance of the Bosphorus in every age. Viewed from the Sea of Marmara end, where the historic city looks most impressive, the Bosphorus appears like a small bay. The rest of the 30 kilometre-long stretch upto the Black Sea appears as consecutive lakes. The first suspension bridge across the Bosphorus was completed in 1973 and the second one in 1988. Only an aerial-view shows that the Bosphorus is actually a strait.

The Bosphorus is a unique "sea-river". The less saline waters of the Black Sea flow towards the Sea of Marmara on the surface, while below the surface, there is another current flowing in the opposite direction. Due to these strong surface currents and the lack of roads, there were few settlements along its shores up until the end of the last century. In the 19th century, besides the small villages, imperial palaces and the summer residences of the wealthy as well as foreign embassies started to appear along its shores. Today, the residential districts along the shores, served by modern roads, suspension bridges and ferry boats, are included within the borders of the metropolis. The strait, which was a river valley in the Ice Age, has a rich marine fauna. It has an average depth of 50 metres and a maximum depth of 112 metres. It is famous for the different kinds of fish caught along its shores as well as in the seas nearby. Different species of fish migrate through these waters seasonally.

Şemsi Paşa Mosque, Üsküdar.

The name "Bosphorus" is derived from mythology and it means the "Cow's Passage". Since it is an easily traversed passage, it facilitated the development of trade and other relations between civilizations in Asia and Europe.

The Bosphorus, its extension, the Golden Horn and the peninsula on which the historic city of Istanbul developed, have been the most sought after location in the world during the last 2,500 years. The campaign of the Argonauts to the Black Sea is the first mythological story about the Bosphorus.

In the 6th century B.C., the Persian armies, in order to cross the Bosphorus easily, tied their boats together side by side, thus forming the first bridge on the Bosphorus. During the "Retrent of Ten Thousands" of Xenophon in the 5th century B.C., their race for Byzantium was mentioned as a very important event.

THE LEANDER'S TOWER

Western sources erroneously state that this is the spot where Leander drowned as he was trying to swim across the strait to be with his lover, Hera. Actually, this incident took place in the Dardanelles, not in the Bosphorus.

This rather small structure, known as the Maiden's Tower (Kız Kulesi), stands on a small islet and has become one of the symbols of Istanbul through the ages, it was used as a watch-tower, a lighthouse and a customs house. Today, it serves as a landmark for ships entering the Bosphorus, and has not changed since the last century.

ÜSKÜDAR

The district near Leander's Tower is an old settlement called Üsküdar. The shortest

route connecting Europe to Asia used to pass through here. The 16th century mosques and the monumental fountain as well as the small Şemsi Paşa Mosque and its schools, built by Sinan on the seashore, are fine examples of Turkish art.

The slopes behind Üsküdar are occupied by the historic Karacaahmet Cemetery where there are many tall and old cypress trees. A little further inland are the Büyük and Küçük Çamlıca hills. These hills, covered with woods, command a magnificent bird's-eye-view of the Princes' Islands, the entrance to the Bosphorus, the old city, the Bosphorus itself and the bridges. A very elegant café built and run by the Turkish Touring Club is on the top of Büyük Çamlıca Hill.

The Bosphorus and Fatih Sultan Mehmet Bridge.

CRUISES ON THE BOSPHORUS

Scheduled ferry boats leave from the piers at the entrance to the Golden Horn and the piers near Dolmabahçe Palace. There are also cruise boats owned by some of the hotels and tour agencies, as well as privately owned and operated smaller boats which organize boat trips on the Bosphorus. These trips run a zigzag course up the Bosphorus towards the Black Sea. Leander's Tower is at the entrance to the Bosphorus, and Dolmabahçe Palace is on the shore opposite Üsküdar. The Çırağan Palace Hotel, along with the Bosphorus Bridge are seen a little further up. The 1,074 metre-long section of the suspension bridge links the two continents. Ortaköy Mosque is next to the foot of the bridge on the European side and Beylerbeyi Palace is next to the foot of the bridge on the Asian Side. Therefore, one gets a chance to see both contemporary and old monuments side by side. Villa Bosphorus, (near Beylerbeyi Palace) where the tours on the Asian shores and the cruises on the Bosphorus stop for a brief rest and shopping, offers a splendid view of Bosphorus Bridge.

Old seaside mansions next to modern residences line both shores of the Bosphorus bordered by hills adorned with different tones of green.

The wide, yellow building with two towers, seen after the first bridge, on the Asian shore going towards the Black Sea, is the famous Kuleli Military Lycee (19th century). The Bay of Bebek is a natural yacht harbour, and the 20th century mosque on the seashore is a small structure exhibiting classical elements. The Bosphorus is a winding waterway which, at each turn, looks like a lake. Its narrowest point, nearly halfway towards the Black Sea, is approximately 800 metres wide. The second bridge on the Bosphorus was completed in 1988 and named after Fatih Sultan Mehmed.

Left: A typical summer day in Kanlıca Bay.

Right: Views from the waterside residences in the Bosphorus shores belonged to the Ottoman era.

The Dolmabahçe Palace.

THE DOLMABAHÇE PALACE

Dolmabahçe Palace, a blend of many European architectural styles, was built between 1843 and 1856 by Karabet Balyan, the chief architect of Sultan Abdülmecid. Ottoman Sultans owned many palaces and pavilions but the Topkapı Palace was the offical residence yet, after the completion of the Dolmabahçe Palace, it was abandoned.

The three-storeyed palace built on a symmetrical plan has 285 rooms and 43 halls. There is a 600 metre-long quay along the sea, and there are two monumental gates one of which is very ornate (the one on the land side). In the middle of the palace surrounded by well-kept gardens, is a large, elevated hall used for meetings and balls. The wing near the entrance was used for the Sultans' receptions and meetings, and the wing on the other side of the ballroom was the Harem. The palace has survived intact with its original decorations, furniture, silk carpets, curtains and everything else. In wealth and magnificence the Dolmabahçe Palace surpasses all other palaces in the world. The walls and ceilings are covered with paintings by the famous artists of the age and with decorations made by using tons of gold. All the furnishings in the major rooms and halls are in different tones of the same colour. Very ornate wood parquet, different in each room, covers the floors. Famous silk and wool carpets of Hereke, some of the finest examples of the Turkish art of carpet weaving, are spread on the floors. Rare handmade object d'art from Europe and the Far East decorate every room in the palace. Brilliant crystal chandeliers, candelabra and fireplaces add to the lavish decor.

Of the six baths in the palace, the one used by the Sultan is made of unusually rich

An interior view of the Dolmabahçe Palace.

looking, specially carved alabaster marble.

The ballroom is the largest of its kind in the world. A 4.5 ton giant-sized chandelier hangs from the 36 metre-high dome. The hall, which is used for important political meetings, balls and signing of treaties, used to be heated by a heating system under the floor until electricity and central heating were installed later. The upper galleries of the hall were reserved for orchestras and the diplomatic corps.

Long hallways lead to the Harem section of the palace where the bedroom of the Sultan, the quarters of his mother, the quarters of the ladies of the Harem and the servants were located. The hallways leading to the Harem have many consecutive doors. More than six hundred valuable paintings hang on the walls in the palace.

The fourth and the last extension of the palace is as large as the Harem and it was used as the quarters of the Crown Prince.

The entrance to this section is from outside the palace complex and today, it houses the Museum of Fine Arts.

Atatürk, founder of the Republic of Turkey, used to stay in this palace during his visits to Istanbul. When he died here in 1938, before his body was taken to Ankara, he laid in state here so that his people could have a chance to pay their last respects to him. All the clocks in the palace were stopped at 9:05 a.m., the time of his death, in memory of this great Turk.

The palace which is a museum, today is open on certain days of the week, and it is one of those historic places in Istanbul that must be seen. There are collections of the precious objets used by the sultans and members of the palace in everyday life and during ceremonies. Some of these have been taken out of storage and are being displayed in two different rooms. Most of these gold, silver and crystal objects, teasets

The Beylerbeyi Palace.

and table settings, dresser sets and other decorative objects are of European origin and each one is a very valuable piece of art.

The rear gardens of the palace and the aviary, along with some of the mansions here, have been renovated and opened to the public.

THE BEYLERBEYİ PALACE

The palace was built on the site of an older wooden mansion between the years 1861-1865. Western motifs along with Turkish and eastern motifs were used to decorate the building. It has two sections: the Harem (for ladies) and the Selamlık (for men). Including the ground floor, the mansion is three-storeyed and has twenty-six rooms and six halls. The small pavillions located at each end of the long quay were for recreation.

There are gardens and terraces with pools behind the building. The Stable Pavilion here is the finest example of its kind, and the pavilions nearby were built before it.

The large mansion has a well-arranged garden and a richly ornamented marble exterior. The large hall in the centre section of the palace has a pool and a spiral staircase. The different artistic styles displayed in the decorations of the hall give it a striking appearance. During its golden days, the mansion was used during the summers and also to accommodate visiting state dignitaries. It has been preserved in its original condition.

Near the imperial seaside mansion is the Villa Bosphorus which is an excellent spot to rest and shop, during the tours of the

Rumeli Hisarı.

RUMELİ HİSARI (THE EUROPEAN FORTRESS)

The city had been beseiged many times before the final seige by the Conqueror in 1453, but had managed to defend itself with the help of the Roman city walls. Even during long seiges, provisions were brought into the city from sea.

Therefore, to prevent any reinforcements and help coming from the Black Sea during the seige, before the final seige started, a fortress was built on the European shore, opposite the other Turkish fortress built earlier on the Asian shore.

Anadolu Hisarı.

The Tarabya Bay and the Grand Tarabya Hotel.

The fortress was completed in an amazingly short time of four months in 1452. This largest and strongest fortress of the Middle Ages was no more important right after the fall of the city.

A fine example of classic Turkish fortress architecture, this impressive fortress is another element adorning the Bosphorus. It was restored in the 1950's and turned into a museum. During the annual Festival of Arts, gardens of the fortress is used as an amphitheatre.

It is viewed best from the Asian shores or from the boats operating on the Bosphorus. The campus of Boğaziçi (Bosphorus) University is spread on the slopes behind the fortress. Robert College, the first American educational institution established outside the United States, used to occupy this campus. In 1967, the college was turned into a university.

ANADOLU HİSARI (THE ANATOLIAN FORTRESS)

The Küçüksu Pavilion and the fortress are situated by a park on the Asian shores of the Bosphorus. It is quite a small fortress built between 1390 and 1391, before the European Fortress on the opposite shore, by Sultan Bayezid, to control the traffic on the Bosphorus, and as a step in the preparations for the final seige of Istanbul. A street passes through this picturesque fortress, situated at a strategic location by the sea, next to a stream that drains into the Bosphorus. There are old wooden houses resting against the small towers of the fortress.

The Kanlıca district, which comes after the fortress, is famous for its yogurt and seaside cafés. The Asian tower of the new "Fatih Bridge" is also situated here.

Shores of the Sarıyer district.

EMİRGÂN AND TARABYA

The old cafés in the Emirgân district along the European shores of the Bosphorus are very popular. Woods covering the hills and slopes make up the Emirgân Municipal Park where there are many lanes for strolling, and three mansions serving as cafés. The annual Tulip Festival is held here each spring.

Below the park is the small Bay of İstinye which, for many years, housed the shipyards. These shipyards were moved to another area, so, the natural beauty of the bay was restored.

A section of the street which extends on the hills from the city to the Bosphorus joins the shore at the Bay of Tarabya, a small yacht harbour. It is flanked by the summer residence of the German Embassy and a beach with modern facilities on one side, and the Grand Tarabya Hotel, a five star hotel, on the other side. Restaurants, serving fish dishes and a variety of Turkish hors d'oeuvres, line the shore.

SARIYER

Summer residences of foreign embassies, restaurants and cafés, line the street that extends along the shore up to the Sarıyer district from where the Black Sea end of the Bosphorus can be seen. The road that starts in Sarıyer leads to the Belgrade Forests on the slopes behind the Büyükdere district, and then continues to Kilyos Beach on the coast of the Black Sea.

Sarıyer is the last stop of the half-day cruises on the Bosphorus. It it also a summer resort which offers a relaxed atmosphere, seaside restaurants and woods in the vicinity.

The last residential district after Sarıyer

Shores of the Rumeli Kavağı.

along the Bosphorus on the European side, is the Rumeli Kavağı district which may be reached either by boat or by car. The rest of the land along the shore after the Rumeli Kavağı district is a restricted area since it belongs to the military. The Anadolu Kavağı district on the Asian side is the last stop for the ferry boats and it is a small fishing village famous for its reasonably priced restaurants. The beaches in Kilyos, which is only 25 km. from central Istanbul are a favourite of lovers of the sea. Accommodation in the village includes a motel and pensions. Istanbul is situated at the junction of different seas. The Bosphorus, the Sea of Marmara and the Black Sea each offers swimmers a unique experience on nearby beaches. Sandy beaches of Şile and Kilyos are about an hour driving distance from the city centre.

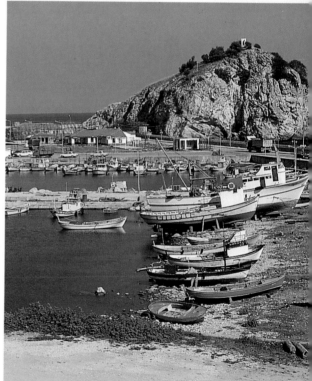

The resort town of Istanbul on the Black Sea Coast.

113

THE PRINCES' ISLANDS

The archipelago known as the Princes' Islands consists of nine various sized islands in the Sea of Marmara and is only an hour away by boat from the pier in the Golden Horn. It is known that during the Byzantine era there were many monasteries here. Some of these were used as imperial summer residences and some were used to house the exiled.

Heybeli Ada is the second largest islands in the archipelago. A small church (the last Byzantine structure built before the fall of Byzantium) dedicated to the Virgin is situated in the inner courtyard of the Naval School on the island. In the beginning of the 19th century, when steamboats started serving the islands, the population of the islands started to increase. Halki Palace Hotel on the Heybeli Island is the oldest hotel in Istanbul. Fully renovated in 1988, the hotel is the best place away from the crowded down-town for perfect rest, swimming and jogging.

The four larger islands are popular summer resorts with ideal picnic areas and beautiful beaches. The islands are heavily populated from May until the end of September, and then become almost desolate in the winter. Scheduled ferry boats serve the islands from the mainland. Throughout the summer and especially on weekends, private boats, yachts and sail-boats anchor in the beautiful coves around every island.

Motor vehicles are not allowed on the islands, the shores of which are lined by seaside mansions, beaches and picnic areas. Horse-drawn carriages are the only means of transportation.

Woods and parks cover the hills on the islands while residences line the northern shores that face the Asian side of Istanbul.

The first island seen from the ferry boat after leaving the pier is the conical shaped, desolate Hayırsız Ada. Next to it is the flat

Typical views from the princes Islands.

Yassı Ada. Although there are military installations on this island, projects are underway to use them for tourism.

Kınalı Ada is the first inhabited island with a beautiful bay in the back, and with beaches opened to the public. Burgaz, with its rocky beaches, comes after Kınalı. There are watersports clubs on the island.

By the square next to the pier at Heybeli Ada and between its two hills, are the buildings of the Naval Schools. Beaches occupy its two beautiful coves. The large buildings of the Orthodox Church were used as a school for the monks in the old days. Halki Palace Hotel on the island is the oldest hotel in Istanbul.

Between Burgaz Ada and Heybeli Ada is a small private island called Kaşık Adası (Spoon Island) due to its shape.

Büyükada is the largest, the most popular and the most famous island in the archipelago. It takes two hours to go around the island (the complete tour) in a horsedrawn carriage. This island with high hills, has two public beaches, one of which is situated in an unusually beautiful cove. The most popular ride on the island follows a course between the mansions in well-kept gardens and through the forests on the hills (the half-tour). Unlike the heavily populated residential areas near the pier, the back of the island is occupied only by desolate, rocky beaches which are ideal harbours for small boats. Fish restaurants and cafés line the seashore near the pier, and there are a few hotels and pensions on the island. On weekends and holidays, people crowd the island for a picnic and to swim.

Left: Merit Halki Palace Hotel: Located on the second largest Prince Island Heybeliada, this historical building has been renovated in 1994. Surrounded by pine trees, the Hotel offers all the services of fivestar Hotel.

Right: Heybeliada, Değirmen region.

The coasts of Heybeliada Pier.

Fish restaurants near the pier in Büyükada.